THE CARROT COOKBOOK

By Audra and Jack Hendrickson

This book is dedicated to our children
and our children's children.

A GARDEN WAY PUBLISHING BOOK

STOREY

STOREY COMMUNICATIONS, INC.
POWNAL, VERMONT 05261

Cover Design by Leslie Morris Noyes
Text Design and Illustrations by Cindy McFarland and Wanda Harper
Cover photo/interior photo: by John M. Kuykendall

Typesetting by Hemmings Publishing

Printed in the United States by Alpine Press
Second Printing, May 1987

Library of Congress Cataloging-in-Publication Data
Hendrickson, Audra.
    The carrot cookbook.

    "A Garden Way Publishing book."
    Includes index.
    1. Cookery (Carrots) I. Hendrickson, Jack.
II. Title
TX803.C35H46   1987   641.6′513   86-45715
ISBN 0-88266-451-4
ISBN 0-88266-433-6 (pbk.)

CONTENTS

ALL YOU EVER WANTED IN A CARROT...

AND MORE!

CARROTS

by David Fedo

In the backyard
surrounded by a ragged hedge
grown neck high
my father and I turn the cool earth over.
Slugs and earthworms dig for cover;
our shovels are merciless.
A neighbor, watching from the hedge,
says there hasn't been a garden here
in twenty years.

(continued on p. 12)

n the beginning, horticultural historians tell us, carrots were white, purple, and yellow, not orange.

Some people thought they were too pretty to eat, and used them for show instead. When the carrot was first introduced into France in the early Middle Ages, people ignored the edible root and grew it for its feathery leaves, which were used to decorate hairstyles, hats, and other items of female apparel. It did not take prudent French housewives long, however, to discover that they could wear their carrots and eat them too.

The root vegetable we know today as the carrot (official name: *Daucus carota)* originated 3,000 years ago in Middle Asia in the area of Afghanistan, and slowly spread into the Mediterranean area.

Before carrots came to Northern Europe to appear in soup kettles and coiffures, they were grown for other purposes. The Greeks used their *karoton* as medicine, not as food. Roman citizens ate their *carotas* only when they weren't feeling well. Carrots were supposed to keep the digestive tract neat and clean, aid in lowering the level of gas in the large intestine, and improve night vision.

But the true glory of carrots was still to come. The orange carrot that was finally developed became the popular choice in most of the world (except Egypt, where they still grow purple carrots). That orange color, promoted and deepened over the generations by gardeners, horticulturists, and commercial growers, has now been linked to beta-carotene content. The deeper the shade of orange, the greater the beta-carotene. And scientists are now discovering the important role this element may play in fighting cancer.

Beta-carotene is the plant pigment that causes carrots and some other vegetables and fruits to be orange. It gets its name from the carrot. In our bodies beta-carotene is converted to vitamin A when and as we need it, and therefore it is defined as that vitamin's "precursor." Surplus amounts are either stored in fat cells or sloughed off as waste. Unlike vitamin A supplements, beta-carotene does not build up to toxic levels in the liver.

Carrots are among the easiest vegetables to grow, to harvest, and to store — see pages 13-20 for tips on growing your own.

And if you don't have the time, space, or inclination to garden, commercially grown carrots are available year-round in your neighborhood store or supermarket, either loose with or without their tops, or pre-weighed and packaged. An added benefit is the fact that their carotene content can increase by as much as 55% during the time between when they are pulled by the commercial grower and the day you buy them.

Whether you buy them or grow them yourself, carrots can be stored fresh, dried, frozen, or canned, and they are basic to hundreds of prepared dishes that are so good to eat it is difficult to believe they could possibly be good for you as well.

The carrot is, in short, the Cook's Best Friend, as you will see when you begin to use the dozens of recipes we have developed, tested, and compiled. They range from Chili con Carrot to Boeuf en Daube, from Carrot Fudge to Clan MacCarrot Broth, from Crustless Carrot Cheesecake to Carrot and Chicken Pilaf.

Bon appetit en bonne santé!
Audra and Jack Hendrickson

THE BETA-CAROTENE FACTOR

CAROTENE
FACTOR

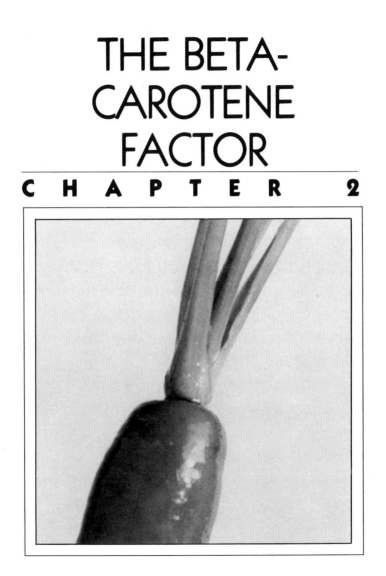

We don't know how beta-carotene helps protect the body against lung cancer. There are many questions that need to be answered by further research. However, there is sufficient evidence to recommend that everyone, especially cigarette smokers, increase consumption of foods rich in beta-carotene.

Lewis Clayton, M.D.
Former Medical Director
American Lung Association

Every generation, every civilization, has been wracked by cancer. Evidences of it have even been found in the autopsied remains of Egyptian pharaohs.

Nearly 70 million Americans now living — close to one-third of the current population of the country — will eventually have cancer. Over the years cancer will hit three out of every four families.

Cancer is unlike the plagues and pestilences of the past. Those epidemic outbreaks of communicable diseases decimated large populations from time to time, spreading from victim to victim like a fire out of control in a high wind. Then they died down as they arose, mysteriously and uncontrollably.

Most cancers, by contrast, have their origins in our cultural behaviour. They are related in some manner to the ways in which we live.

Although scientists are still exploring the causes of cancer, it seems that we may "catch" the disease from smoking cigarettes, from pollution in our environment, or from eating the wrong things.

In fact, the foods we eat are at the heart of the medical and scientific world's current efforts to contain, to control, and to prevent, if possible, the cancers that are killing us in increasing numbers.

Some investigators have estimated that the foods we eat are responsible for 30 to 40 percent of cancers in men and 60 percent of cancers in women. Others have recently suggested that a significant proportion of deaths due to cancer could be *prevented* by a change in the diet, and that this would have the greatest effect on the incidence of cancers of the stomach and large bowel (and to a lesser extent, on cancers of the breast, the endometrium, and the lung).

Of course, quitting smoking is the most important step in prevention of lung cancer. An astonishingly large number of this country's nearly half million cancer fatalities have been traced to cigarette smoking.

Beta-carotene, the plant pigment (named after the carrot) that causes carrots and some other vegetables and fruits to be orange, is being recommended as an important natural element that may protect human beings from cancer.

THE BETA-CAROTENE FACTOR

The presence of beta-carotene in our systems in adequate amounts helps ensure healthy *epithelial tissue*. Epithelial tissue comprises the inner linings and outer coverings of our bodies where 90% of the cancers that kill us — the *carcinomas* — occur:

🔥 The skin and eyes

🔥 Stomach, intestine and bladder linings

🥕 Lining of urinary tract

🥕 Lining of reproductive organs

🥕 Inner surface of the lungs

🥕 Inner surface of bronchial passages

🥕 Inner surface of nasal passages

🥕 Inner surfaces of throat and mouth

Beta-carotene is one of a family of chemical substances called *carotenoids,* the original source of all vitamin A. The one we call beta-carotene is converted in our bodies to vitamin A and is one of the major sources of that nutrient. Since beta-carotene is an earlier phase of vitamin A, it is called a "precursor" or "prototype" vitamin.

When we eat vegetables or fruits containing beta-carotene, it is taken from the digestive tract into the bloodstream and a portion is deposited in tissues such as skin and body fat. As our bodies require it, beta-carotene (*pro*vitamin A) is converted into *dietary* vitamin A.

What the body needs is used immediately. A back-up supply is stored in the liver and the rest of the unused beta-carotene remains dormant in the tissues or is disposed of by the body's normal processes of elimination if the accumulation becomes too great.

(We also ingest vitamin A "preformed" when we eat the flesh of animals that have eaten beta-carotene-containing plants, or the produce of those animals, such as milk, eggs, butter and cheese. Unlike provitamin A, this preformed version can be dangerous if eaten in too great quantities, as is the case with vitamin A supplements.)

RESEARCH STUDIES. One of the most famous of the studies supporting the hypothesis that some cancers are diet-related took place in Chicago between 1957 and 1977. Two thousand workers of the Western Electric Company plant there — both smokers and non-smokers — reported on their eating habits over twenty years. At the end of the study it was discovered that the subjects who ate the most beta-carotene-rich foods were many times less apt to develop lung cancers than those who ate the least beta-carotene-rich foods.

Many other studies are on record that verify the Western Electric Company research. There are also numerous laboratory experiments with animals to support it. A particularly convincing one conducted in 1970 showed the effect of beta-carotene on cancer in general: Laboratory mice lived out their normal life spans in good health when treated with beta-carotene *after twice being infected with lethal cases of cancer.*

In the Spring of 1982 the National Research Council reported in "Diet, Nutrition and Cancer" that beta-carotene's positive effect as an inhibitor of cancer is consistent with research indicating that it "has significant capacity to inhibit carcinogenesis in epithelial cells." (See Appendix, page 155, for the NRC's "Interim Dietary Guidelines.")

To date there have been well over 300 research studies involving beta-carotene and its other form, vitamin A. The data from these studies are on file with the National Cancer Institute (NCI).

Eleven out of twenty-six "chemoprevention intervention" studies currently sponsored by the NCI are beta-carotene projects. They include the biggest experiment ever conducted in the United States on carotenoids such as beta-carotene. Nearly 22,000 male physicians 40 to 84 years of age with no previous evidence of cancer are participating. Half the doctors take a high-dosage capsule (30 milligrams) of beta-carotene every other day, and half take a placebo. The study will be completed in 1987.

Based on previous studies, many researchers expect beta-carotene to be confirmed as one of the most powerful preventive weapons to date against fatal cancers.

FACTS TO REMEMBER ABOUT CARROTS AND BETA-CAROTENE

Vegetables are the chief source of vitamin A for North Americans and Europeans. About half of the vitamin A available to us in food comes from the beta-carotene found in certain vegetables and fruits. Of all the fruits and vegetables, carrots are richest in beta-carotene, the "precursor" or "provitamin" (source) of vitamin A.

In days of yore, deep reddish-orange carrot juice was often added to pale yellow home-made butter in order to make it look more appetizing. Now beta-carotene is often added to pale yellow manufactured margarine for the same reason.

Beta-carotene is a dark red crystalline plant pigment that gives a deep-yellow color to plants such as carrots and sweet potatoes. In deep-green plants such as broccoli and parsley the color can't be seen because of the chlorophyll that makes them green.

One single dark orange carrot can supply enough beta-carotene to provide our total daily allowance requirement of vitamin A.

Grownups who don't get enough of the vitamin A provided by beta-carotene often suffer from night blindness and extreme sensitivity to sunlight glare. Their fingernails split, peel, and become ridged; their hair becomes dry, brittle and dull; and their skin develops blemishes, wrinkles, and dries out.

Children who don't get enough vitamin A are more susceptible to infections than those who do; their growth can be retarded; and their bones and teeth do not develop as they should. Extremely severe vitamin A deficiency in young people can result in xerophthalmia which can cause blindness.

The beta-carotene that carrots contain, which is converted by the body into vitamin A, is necessary for night vision. It also helps prevent susceptibility to some eye infections.

It is estimated that vitamin A deficiency causes some 80 thousand of the Third World's very young to go totally blind every year. Insufficient vitamin A is known to be the primary cause of blindness in American children as well.

Growing scientific evidence indicates that there may be an inverse relationship between the risk of cancer and the eating of foods that contain vitamin A (e.g., liver) or its precursors (e.g., the carotenoids in green and yellow vegetables). But so far most of the data do not show whether the effects are due to carotenoids, to vitamin A itself, or to some other constituent of these foods, according to investigators.

In addition to their beta-carotene bounty, carrots are good providers of fiber, potassium and other minerals, yet there are fewer than 50 calories in a cupful.

When buying carrots, choose those that are firm to the touch and rich in color — a deep, rich orange. *The deeper the orange color of the carrot, the greater the beta-carotene content.*

The richness of orange color in a vegetable or fruit is usually an indication of the amount of beta-carotene a food contains. But this is not always the case. Oranges, for instance, have little or no beta-carotene, despite their color.

Carrots have more beta-carotene content when they are mature than they do when they are young — some varieties up to twice as much.

The beta-carotene in cooked vegetables is more easily assimilated by the body than that in raw vegetables.

Dr. Richard Shekelle, who conducted the Western Electric study (see page 8), says everyone should eat a couple of servings every day of fruits and vegetables high in beta-carotene, along with a little butter or some other animal fat to aid absorption of the beta-carotene.

In cases of extremely heavy consumption of beta-carotene-rich foods, the skin can take on a slight but harmless orange tint. Skin color returns to normal in a short period of time when the diet is adjusted. (Many people find the tint attractive — like a sun tan.)

CARROT CULTURE

CHAPTER 3

CARROTS (continued)

We plant carrots in even rows.
The sun warms us as we work.
My father's shirt is off;
I can see the patches of prickly white
hair on his back.
The seeds snuggle down easily.
I rake away the clumps of grass
and stones,
turn on the sprinkler.
My father dozes in a canvas lawn chair.

(continued p. 22)

One of our neighbors invited us to help ourselves to the remainder of his carrot crop one autumn.

"Come on over," he said. "We've gotten as many carrots as we can use from the garden, and there are still several bushels left in the ground."

"Several bushels" was right.

When we started to pull carrots, we could hardly believe our eyes. The rows of plants had obviously seldom been thinned. Crowding each other sideways in the rows, which were about two feet apart, the carrots lined up as many as five or six abreast. They were so cramped, they hardly had to be pulled. They seemed to burst out of the ground and into our hands with sighs of relief.

The soil in which they had been grown was perfect for carrot culture — light and loose, rich and nourishing, well drained and free of rocks and weeds. In one morning, we pulled four bushels of the best carrots we have ever seen in our lives. The skins were smooth, firm and crisp, and the roots were deep orange in color, right through to the core.

The challenge of dealing with four bushels of carrots was a big factor in the genesis of this book. In short order, we learned to incorporate carrots into every part of our menus, from breakfast dishes to late-night suppers and desserts.

And we discovered that one can never grow too many carrots....

While the common carrot is orange enough, most would think, and most uncommon when it comes to beta-carotene content, there are now "super carrots" that make the ones we're used to look as pale in comparison as their ancient ancestors. These new hybrids contain 40 to 70 percent more beta-carotene than ordinary carrots. The new varieties — for example, Luckies Gold, A-Plus and Danvers Gold — are deep orange in color. Just one of these super carrots can contain more than enough beta-carotene to provide the daily allowance of vitamin A recommended for adults by the National Academy of Sciences. These new carrot types (now available for commercial and home gardeners) are just the first of what horticultural scientists expect to be a long line of royal orange root crops.

Whether "super" or "ordinary," the carrot is a biennial plant that normally requires two growing seasons, with a cool rest period between, in order to complete its life cycle from germination to seed production. The home gardener, of course, plants carrots for food, not for seed, and so has little awareness of the phases the plant goes through as it passes from one stage to the next in its growth cycle.

But on the vast farms in California or in Crécy,

France, where many of the world's carrots are grown, the growing of carrots is all business and a different story entirely.

Modern machines sow the seeds in bands to give room for plant development without the need for thinning, but with minimum area for weed development. During that first season, a circle of bright feathery green leaves develops. The carrots are not harvested but are left in the ground to develop and grow strong and full of nutrients.

After the growing season is past, the food energy stored in the root is called on by Mother Nature to provide the nourishment for the next phase, the production of seeds.

During the second season, the plant puts up large flower stalks on thick stems, and their tips blossom into plate-shaped clusters of tiny white or pink flowers resembling the blossoms of Queen Anne's lace. These flowers produce the seeds.

GROWING CONDITIONS

Because they prefer cool to moderate temperatures, carrots aren't grown in summer in the warmer regions of the world. Carrot-growing experts tell us that several conditions affect not only their looks, but more importantly, their beta-carotene content. For the highest beta-carotene, carrots should be grown during the months when the days are longest, where average temperatures are between 60 and 70 degrees F, with alternat-

WILD CARROT

Queen Anne's lace ("wild carrot") is thought by many botanists to be the aboriginal ancestor of the domestic carrot of today. The two are not on speaking terms, however, since the wild ones are regarded as bothersome weeds never welcome in areas where domestic carrots are cultivated. Wild carrots are thin, wiry and bitter, with no food value. Like most pests of whatever genus, they seem to be always trying to move in where they are not wanted, by one means or another — in this case, by cross-pollination, causing the true carrots to deteriorate in quality over time.

ing warm days and cool nights. The soil should be deep, rich, loosely packed, well drained, and free of rocks.

Extremes of temperature are especially hard on the young plants, which may be badly injured or killed by heat or cold. Too much heat tends to shorten the roots of long varieties, and too *little* warmth tends to make the roots longer, more slender and paler in color than they should be. "Paler in color" means deficient in beta-carotene.

One variety or another, however, can be grown with some success at some season of the year almost anywhere that other vegetables are grown, and they are among the easiest vegetables to grow, to harvest and to store.

VARIETIES

Dozens of varieties of carrots are grown and marketed in this country. There are several basic or "parent" types that differ considerably in length, diameter and shape (see diagram below), but they are generally similar in taste, color and other carrot virtues, raw or cooked.

When making choices for your garden, keep in mind your soil conditions and your taste preferences. Longer roots require deeper soil; the flavor spectrum of carrots ranges from bland to strong.

As you see by the diagram, the long, more slender carrots are the varieties you are most apt to find on your supermarket produce counter. Imperator leads the parade as the "standard market carrot."

The other varieties are also tasty, and are easier for the home gardener to grow, primarily because they thrive in shallower friable soil than do the market varieties.

The round carrots (not shown) will do well even when planted close together in quite shallow soil. These are marketed under such trade names as Planet, Gold Nugget, and Kundulus. There are a considerable number of hybrids, some of them "propietary" — available from only one source under a given trade name.

The three new types of super carrot — Danvers Gold, A-Plus and Luckies Gold — are so far unmatched regarding beta-carotene content and they have been rated for taste as preferable to many other types of commercially grown carrots.

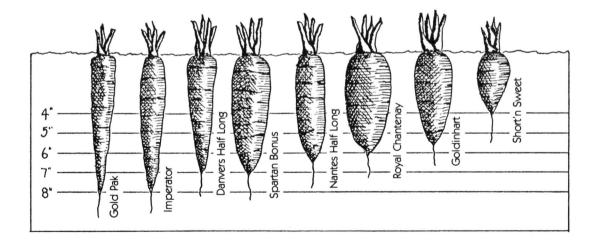

COMMON CARROT VARIETIES

VARIETY	DESCRIPTION
HYBRID ROYAL CROSS	excellent taste quality; long, tapering, smooth roots
SCARLET NANTES	excellent flavor; long, slender, smooth roots with blunt ends
PIONEER	texture fine and sweet, with excellent flavor; long slender roots
HYBRID LANCE	flavor sweet and excellent; long, slender smooth roots
SHORT 'N SWEET	texture firm and excellent, with excellent sweet flavor; short smooth roots
ROYAL CHANTENAY	texture firm with good flavor; roots long, smooth and slightly tapered
SPARTAN SWEET HYBRID	fine texture, flavor sweet and delicious; long, large diameter roots
IMPERATOR	fine texture and quite good flavor; long, slender roots
SPARTAN PREMIUM HYBRID	fine texture and good flavor; long roots of the Danvers type
SPARTAN CLASSIC HYBRID	fine texture and good flavor; smooth Nantes-type roots
PARK'S MUNCHY HYBRID	flavor quite good; long, slender roots
NANTES CORELESS	fairly good taste; large diameter medium length roots
SPECIAL NANTES 616	bland flavor; roots of the Nantes type
TOUCHON	fine texture with mild flavor; short Nantes-type roots
TOUCHON DELUXE	fine texture with good sweetness and flavor; long Nantes-like roots
GOLD KING	good texture and strong flavor; smooth Danvers-type roots
FINGER STICK	good texture and bland flavor; smooth Nantes-type roots

VARIETY	DESCRIPTION
LITTLE FINGERS	bland flavor and good texture; long Nantes-type roots
BABY ORANGE	good texture and good flavor; small Nantes-type roots.
TINY SWEET	mild flavor; short Danvers-type roots.

If you need help in locating a source of supply for seeds for the super carrot or any of the varieties described above, get in touch with the nearest Agricultural Extension Service office or seed supply company.

They are now, or soon will be, available in your area. Ask your nurseryman about them when you next buy seeds, and check with the produce counter manager at your supermarket as to when you can expect the super carrot in the display bins.

HOW TO GROW CARROTS

PREPARATION. Turn your soil with spade or roto-tiller. Fertilizer should be worked in well ahead of planting so that the earth has time to assimilate it. For sweet-tasting carrots your soil must have sufficient lime, humus and potash. Nitrogen-based and organic-type fertilizers work well, but follow directions carefully, as too much nitrogen will cause poor flavor. Avoid using fresh manure, as it makes carrots grow hairy roots.

The long, slim carrot varieties grow best in light, sandy soil worked to a depth of up to 10 inches. Short and chunky types thrive better in richer, heavier soils, with the soil worked to a depth that suits the estimated length of the mature root (see diagram on p. 15).

PLANTING. Plant carrots as early as possible in the spring — as soon as the soil is dry enough to work. The seeds may be planted in old-style narrow rows, or in the wide rows that are more often preferred today.

If you choose the narrow-row technique leave four to five inches between the rows for easier cultivation. Make shallow furrows and sprinkle the seeds in them. Next, sift fine soil, peat, sawdust, sand, or a mixture of all four over the seeds. Otherwise simply draw the furrow edges in to cover the seeds as you go.

Wide-row planting offers a number of advantages: (1) You may get two to three times more produce per square foot than with narrow rows by wasting less space between rows and by having fewer walk-paths; (2) wide rows provide a continual harvest since some plants mature faster than others and pulling the carrots as they "come to size" allows room and time for the slower growers to reach their own peak; (3) wide rows mean less weeding since the greens grow thickly to shade each other and to smother weeds; (4) the soil stays cooler and more moist, and the plants protect each other from sun and wind damage; (5) planting is easier and harvesting, too, since you can reach more plants from one position.

If you decide to plant in wide-rows, scatter your seed on a strip of loosened soil about 15 inches wide (a garden rake's width). Cover over with a quarter-inch of fine soil. If you suspect you have sown too thickly, pull a rake about one-half to three-quarters of an inch into the soil once across the row.

Carrot seeds are pretty fine, and it is not the easiest thing in the world to keep from planting too many. One trick is to mix fine soil or sand with the seed before planting to allow for better spacing. Another is to use a perforated shaker such as a salt or pepper shaker with some of the holes taped over. Or you can mix one cup of *unused* coffee grounds with a package of carrot seeds for spacing and to help repel root maggots.

Modern gardeners know that it is wise to "companion-plant" for best results. Good companion plants for carrots include onions, leeks, and herbs such as rosemary, wormwood and sage, which repel the carrot fly. Black salsify, sometimes called the oyster plant, is also effective in repelling the carrot fly.

Other carrot "friends" include tomatoes, leaf lettuce, chives, red radishes, beans, peas, brussels sprouts, peppers, and cabbage. Carrots, in turn, are beneficial to the growth of other plants, such as peas.

The "enemies" of the carrot include dill, celery, parsnips — and Queen Anne's lace!

If you don't have a backyard big enough to handle a garden, you can grow round carrots in window boxes or on your patio. Yes, *round* carrots! They're about the size of small tomatoes. Check with your nursery supply store, or look in seed catalogs for availability of seeds.

Note: For an unusual carrot patch, you can build grow-boxes, the kind the folks who came on the "Mayflower" built around their houses at Plymouth Plantation. The grow-boxes Mistresses Warren, Doty and Cooke used were like 12-inch-deep cold-frames without the covers, filled with the best soil they could find.

CULTIVATING. Do not let even one single weed make itself at home in your carrot patch while the seedlings are small. As the carrots grow, their leaves will shade the soil between the plants and cut down on weed growth. Until then your carrot seedlings depend on you for protection.

To get started right, plant a few icicle radishes in your carrot row. Carrots are slow to germinate; the radishes will come up quickly and discourage weed starts. They will also provide an early harvest. As you pull the radishes, extra space will be opened up for your carrots.

Weed by hand instead of with a hoe or scratcher to prevent accidental damage to the roots of the tender seedlings.

To cut down on weed growth and improve carrot growth, mulch between the plants with some kind of compost material such as leaves, grass clippings, or fine bark. As they decay into the soil, these materials will provide extra nourishment for the growing carrots. Mulching also helps the soil stay moist. Additional sprinklings of coffee grounds on the soil during the growing season will help to discourage carrot pests.

For the best carrots, cut down on the amount of water you give them as they get close to full size in order to keep the roots from cracking and splitting.

Thinning is especially important with carrots in order to assure that the crop you harvest achieves its optimum size and quality. *As a general rule, thin your crop to two inches between the seedlings when they are finger thick and then later to four inches between plants when they are obviously beginning to crowd each other and compete for water and nutrients.*

(If you have planted wide rows, a preliminary thinning may be done when the seedlings are small with careful rake strokes through the row. Later on you should thin by hand as prescribed above.)

If you have extra space in your garden you can replant carrot thinnings. Tuck them in gently and keep them well watered until they have adjusted to their new location. Be aware, however, that replanting sometimes results in double roots.

A delicious alternative to replanting: the "fingerlings" from your second thinning will make tasty table fare, cooked whole, or in salads, raw and crunchy.

HARVESTING. Some experts hold that carrots should be pulled before they are even half-grown, contending that the saying "the biggest isn't the best" applies more to carrots than to any other crop. We know, however, that the more mature the carrot, the more the beta-carotene it contains, so we *never* thin ours expressly to eat.

Early carrots *may* be harvested when the root tops are barely visible above ground. As carrots push up out of the ground, cover the tips with soil.

The largest carrots will be beneath the darkest, greenest tops. This is one way to tell if a carrot has a root without having to pull it up and see. Remove the tops when harvesting to prevent wilting.

Carrots are said by many gardening experts to be at their taste peak when they are about the same diameter as a quarter. However, research has shown that as a carrot ages, its beta-carotene content increases. Thus, older and larger carrots are your best health bet even if they are less tender than the smaller ones. Since we know the beta-carotene they contain is easier to assimilate when they are cooked, carrots no longer have to be harvested and eaten when they are young and tender to be at their best.

Most varieties of carrots will be big enough to harvest after two months, but some will take nearly three months. Leave them in the ground to get bigger and sweeter — and to be on hand when you want them fresh — until they are in danger of freezing.

You will harvest about one pound of carrots for each foot of row that you have planted.

COMMON CARROT ENEMIES

Carrots are not susceptible to many diseases, but they do sometimes get blight, root scab, aster yellows, and motley dwarf disease. Most such problems can be avoided by *companion planting* as described above, that is, planting with other vegetables and herbs that are not susceptible to the same maladies, or by use of *organic* pesticides. *Chemical treatments are not recommended.* They are harmful to animal and bird life and can be to you.

If diseases persist, you may be well advised to move the location of your carrot patch for the next growing season. Alternating plant bed locations each year is called "crop rotation" by farmers and not only helps control diseases but restores nutrients temporarily depleted by too many plantings of one type of crop.

Insect enemies of carrots include cutworms, rusty banded aphids and tulip aphids, petrobia mites, root-knot nematodes, and wireworms. Unused coffee grounds mixed into the soil when planting will discourage root pests as noted above; and coffee grounds sprinkled later among the growing plants will help drive away leaf eaters. A mulch of oak leaves will repel cutworms. Collars of paper or cans with top and bottom cut out and fitted around the plant stems are also recommended by some horticulturalists (but not practical in a big planting). Hand-picking of the pesky invaders remains the most reliable method.

Again, carrots are hardy plants and do not have many plant diseases or pest enemies. Caught early, infestations will not likely be unmanageably large.

STORING CARROTS. There are many ways to store carrots: (1) In the garden, by heavily mulching the top and sides of the row with at least a foot of hay or leaves. Mulch heavily or they'll lose their crunch; eat soon after digging or they'll spoil. (2) In the refrigerator, if you have room. They'll keep for several months in plastic bags. (3) In a box, in a cool room. Dig the carrots, let them dry for an hour in the sun, snip off the tops. Place a four-inch layer of dampened peat moss in the bottom of a big box. Put in a single layer of carrots, keeping them two inches from the sides of the box. Cover with a half-inch layer of dampened peat moss, then fill the box, alternating layers of peat moss and carrots. Top with six inches of peat moss. (4) Place in plastic trash bags in which holes have been punched. Store in a cool root cellar, or a basement, closet, or garage. (5) Pack the carrots in a barrel or bin full of sand or sawdust. In the days before refrigeration and canning, they were kept usable like this until the middle of the next growing season.

If none of the above methods is convenient or appealing, you may choose to can and/or freeze them. Follow directions included in the manuals for your freezer or canning apparatus.

USING CARROTS & THIS BOOK

C H A P T E R 4

CARROTS (continued)

Our only crop will be carrots.
Long ago
In this same but different earth
we grew carrots
as sweet as apples.
They were harvested in September,
stored in a big crock in the cellar.
In such silence
our carrots
each year
overcame Minnesota winters.

Reprinted by permission of Commonweal Magazine

Mature, deeply orange carrots are preferred by processors because they are more attractive than paler ones, and this preference accounts for the high beta-carotene values to be found in frozen, canned and dried carrot products.

Grated carrots are a popular partner in cole slaw. Shred them over other fresh vegetable salads, too.

Carrots can be cooked in many ways, including boiling, blanching, steaming, braising, frying, sautéing, baking, deep-frying, microwaving, and pressure cooking.

Onion, celery leaves, and parsley are excellent flavor companions for carrots.

It isn't necessary to peel homegrown carrots unless they simply cannot be brushed clean. Just wash them carefully, brush the soil out of the little eyes, and trim off the tops and the ends of the roots.

Keep a container of carrot sticks in your refrigerator for between-meal snacking, and include them in salads and on relish trays. They go well with nearly every kind of dip, and they are always the first thing to be eaten up.

If you do prefer to peel your carrots, a common potato peeler will remove the minimum amount of carrot necessary to do the job. The only time we scrape carrots is when they are too small to be held comfortably and safely for paring.

Form cooked, mashed carrots into a ring and fill it with any other cooked fresh vegetable for an attractive dish.

Grated carrots can be frozen without any special preparation (such as blanching or steaming), and can be thawed for use fresh in salads, or added to recipes for cooked or baked dishes, including breads, cookies, cakes and pies.

Add chopped carrots to tuna salad or taco filling for extra crunch and color.

Make an easy carrot jam by cooking diced carrots until they are soft, adding sugar to taste, and flavoring with grated lemon or orange peel. (Keep in mind while adding the sugar that the carrots themselves are quite sweet; at least five to ten percent of their bulk is sugar.) Refrigerate the jam and use it within two weeks.

Glaze carrots in honey, brown sugar, or pancake syrup and serve them with poultry dishes for a change of taste.

Use carrots regularly as an ingredient in cookies and cakes. Grate them and add them to your batter just before you finish the mixing process.

Add raw carrots wrapped in plastic to lunch bags and boxes.

Carrots are useful for lending body, color and flavor — to say nothing of beta-carotene — to soups of all kinds.

Always add a few carrots to roast meat dishes for nutrition, looks and taste. Improve tomato-based dishes with grated or puréed carrots.

Combine steamed carrots with peas and new potatoes in a creamy white sauce for a delicious and easy side dish.

Carrot bread is a great snack and makes delicious sandwiches when teamed with peanut butter, chicken, or ham.

Leftover cooked carrots can be puréed, poured into ice-cube trays, and frozen for later use in soups, stews and sauces.

Combine carrots with pineapple rounds, orange wedges, peach slices, pear quarters, or apricot halves — along with a complementary gelatin — for an easy salad with good taste and beta-carotene benefits.

For the best toast ever, make a loaf of Staff of Life Carrot Yeast Bread (see p. 115), slice thin, and toast at low heat until crisp.

There are 12–13 *small* (6–7") carrots in a pound. One small carrot, grated, makes about ⅓ of a cup; coined, it makes ¼–⅓ of a cup.

There are six *medium* (7–8") carrots in a pound. One medium carrot, grated, makes about 1 cup; coined, it makes 2/3–3/4 of a cup.

There are five *medium-large* (9–10") carrots in a pound. One medium-large carrot, grated, makes about 1¼ cups; coined, it makes just under a cup.

There are four *large* (11–12") carrots in a pound. One large carrot, grated, makes about 1 1/3 cups; coined, it makes one cup.

Small carrots are milder and more tender than large carrots, which are usually more flavorful and filled with more beta-carotene.

Cut carrots into long strips and cook them with green or wax beans, onions, broccoli, or cauliflower pieces.

When we use carrots we have grown, pulled fresh from soil we have prepared, handled by no one but us, we just wash them carefully, and use them without peeling. But, when we are using carrots that have been grown, shipped, stored, and then offered for sale in supermarket produce bins, we peel them before we use them. The amount of carrot lost in the peeling is very small, and we have never seen anything anywhere to indicate that there is more beta-carotene in the peeling than in the layer just underneath it.

We have found that the best way to peel a carrot — using a standard U-handled potato peeler — is to grasp the carrot about halfway along its length in the palm of the hand, holding it at a slightly oblique angle with the tip pointed toward your other hand. Pull the peeler toward you in long smooth strokes to remove the skin from the tip half, then reverse the carrot and finish by stroking away from the tip, removing the peeling at the crown end. Finally, cut off the tip and as much of the crown as is necessary to remove the base of the carrot top.

Small carrots are more easily scraped than peeled, using a standard paring knife. Hold the carrot by the crown end with the tip pointing toward you. Grasp the paring knife so that your index finger is extended along the top of the blade (the blunt side of the blade) and scrape towards you. Reverse the carrot and hold it by the tip end as you scrape the skin off the crown end. Remove the leaf base and the tip of the carrot and it is ready to use.

Garnishes made from carrots add color and interest to party platters, salad plates, relish trays, desserts, and casseroles. They can be as simple as a dusting of grated carrot over a salad or casserole, or as complicated as figures carved to carry out a dinner motif. Somewhere in between those two extremes are carrot curls, ringlets, bows, loops and rosettes. They're quite easy to make: Using a potato peeler, cut very thin strips the length of a long slender carrot. Now, pretend you are going to decorate a gift box and shape the strips just as you would if you were using a ribbon. When you have the shape you want, secure the ends with a length of toothpick, place in a container of ice water and chill until crisp.

According to the U.S. Department of Agriculture, the amount of beta-carotene in a particular variety of carrot increases with maturity. For example, Imperator, a leading variety, has a vitamin A value of about 11,000 International Units per 100 grams (or a beta-carotene value of 18,730 International Units for the same weight) when it is ready for the produce bin at your neighborhood market. But when it is more mature, the same carrot could have almost twice as much beta-carotene and vitamin A value.

If you don't want to freeze or can carrots, but want to have some on hand at all times, either dry them yourself or stock up on the dried carrot flakes available in the baby food section of most supermarkets. (We also keep several jars of puréed car-rot baby food in our pantry for use in soups, stews, sauces, meat loaf, and the like.)

Whenever a recipe calls for butter or margarine, either may be used, depending on your personal preference, health concern, or taste. Some will want to avoid butter because it contains cholesterol; others will want to use butter because of its flavor. Some nutritionists advise eating carrots in conjunction with small amounts of animal fat in order to facilitate its absorption by the body, since beta-carotene-derived vitamin A is one of the fat-soluble vitamins.

At high altitudes, cake recipes should be adjusted as follows: At 3000 feet and above, increase the oven temperature by 25 degrees. Above 5000 feet, reduce baking powder amounts by ⅛ to ¼ teaspoon for each teaspoon called for in the recipe; decrease sugar by one or two tablespoons per cup; and increase the flour by two to three tablespoons per cup. (Please note that these adjustments are general. If you have any questions about specific requirements at a particular altitude, check with the county extension service or ask an experienced cook from your area.)

Unless otherwise specified, carrots, potatoes, squash and the like are to be peeled for use in the recipes.

TONICS
BEVERAGES
& COCKTAILS
C H A P T E R   5

There is hardly anything in this world more completely delicious — or better for you — than a glass of fresh carrot juice made from just-pulled, sweet, crisp carrots. It is, in effect, liquid beta-carotene, and it has become very popular with health food promoters in recent years as more and more people have turned to natural foods for good nutrition and good taste.

Carrot juice is without question the star of the health beverage show. It's hard to improve upon, but different supporting casts can make for dramatic new experiences. Here are some suggestions:

Combine carrot juice with other vegetable juices such as beet, celery, brussels sprouts, spinach or tomato to make healthful tonics. Spices to add piquance to the mixtures include paprika, sage, horseradish, and pepper and salt. You might also want to stir in dashes of onion juice, lemon juice, or Worcestershire sauce.

Mix carrot juice with any of your favorite fruit juices — or fruit juice combinations. Carrots are almost as naturally sweet as many fruits, such as apples, pears, apricots, pineapples, peaches and oranges.

The quality of the juice or tonic or cocktail depends on the quality of the ingredients used in making it. We have found that our homegrown super carrots make such superb carrot juice (it's almost criminally delicious!) that we can't bear to add *anything* to it.

If we don't have homegrown carrots on hand, we make our favorite carrot tonics, beverages and cocktails with strained or puréed *cooked* carrots. They have the added advantage of containing the fiber that is missing from raw carrot juice.

CHILLED CARROT CREAM

PREPARATION: 5-10 MINUTES   **SERVES: TWO**

¾ cup carrot juice or purée
½ cup chilled cream
½ teaspoon finely minced parsley

Dash celery seed
Crushed ice

   Combine all ingredients in a shaker and serve
at once.

3-C TONIC

PREPARATION: 5-10 MINUTES   **SERVES: TWO**

1 cup carrot juice or purée
¼ cup cucumber juice
1 tablespoon vegetable oil (optional)
½ tablespoon cider vinegar

Salt to taste
Dash paprika
Crushed ice

   Combine ingredients over cracked ice in a tall
glass and serve at once.

TONIQUE DOUCEUR

PREPARATION: 5-10 MINUTES   **SERVES: TWO**

¾ cup carrot juice
½ cup celery juice
Dash onion juice

Pinch salt
Crushed ice

   In a pitcher or a shaker blend the ingredients.
Pour the mixture over the crushed ice and serve.

TONIQUE ROYALE

PREPARATION: 5-10 MINUTES   **SERVES: TWO**

¼ cup carrot juice or purée
½ cup beet juice

⅛ cup celery juice
Dash onion juice

Mix ingredients in a pitcher or a shaker. Pour the mixture over crushed ice. Serve immediately.

DOUBLE ORANGE DRINK

PREPARATION: 5-10 MINUTES   **SERVES: TWO**

¾ cup carrot juice or purée
½ cup orange juice
½ teaspoon sugar (optional)
Dash lemon juice

Dash salt
Crushed ice
Orange slices

Thoroughly blend the carrot juice or purée, orange juice, sugar, lemon juice and salt. Pour this mixture over the crushed ice, garnish with orange slices, and serve at once.

MULLED CARROT DRINK

PREPARATION: 5-10 MINUTES   **SERVES: TWO**

1 cup carrot juice or purée
1 cup tomato juice

Dash Worcestershire sauce
Pinch celery seed

Combine all ingredients, heat and serve.

PINEAPPLE PUNCH

PREPARATION: 5-10 MINUTES   **SERVES: TWO**

1 cup carrot juice or purée
1 cup pineapple juice

Crushed ice
Lime wedges

Blend the carrot juice or purée with the pineapple juice and pour the mixture over crushed ice in chilled glasses. Garnish with lime wedges and serve at once.

SUMMER SIPPER

PREPARATION: 5-10 MINUTES   **SERVES: TWO**

¾ cup carrot juice or purée
½ cup apricot nectar
¼ cup pineapple juice

Crushed or cubed ice
Dash of nutmeg

In a pitcher or shaker blend the carrot juice or purée with the apricot nectar and pineapple juice and pour the mixture over the crushed or cubed ice. Sprinkle with nutmeg and serve.

YOGURT PLUS

PREPARATION: 5-10 MINUTES   **SERVES: TWO**

Carrot juice or purée
Lemon, banana, orange or plain low-fat yogurt

Mint or parsley sprigs

Combine equal parts carrot juice or purée and yogurt. Blend well and serve, garnished with a sprig of mint or parsley.

Beverages and drinks featuring carrot juice or carrot purée can also be combined with liquors and liqueurs for some unusual cocktails and after-dinner drinks. Some of our favorites follow.

CARROT COCKTAIL

PREPARATION: 5-10 MINUTES   **SERVES: TWO**

½ cup fruit cocktail nectar
½ cup carrot juice or purée
4 jiggers white rum

6 cubes sugar
Crushed ice
Orange slices

Blend nectar, carrot juice or purée and rum thoroughly and pour the mixture over the sugar cubes and crushed ice in tall chilled glasses. Add an orange slice to each and serve.

CARROT COLLINS

PREPARATION: 5-10 MINUTES   **SERVES: TWO**

½ cup carrot juice or purée
½ cup vodka or gin
1 cup tonic water or collins mix

Cubed or crushed ice
2 slices lemon or lime

Combine the carrot juice or purée with the vodka or gin and the tonic water or collins mix in a pitcher or shaker and stir or shake until all the ingredients are well blended.

Pour the mixture over cubed or crushed ice in tall chilled drink glasses and add a slice of lemon or lime to each as you serve it.

ALEXANDRA

PREPARATION: 5-10 MINUTES   **SERVES: TWO**

4 jiggers sweet cream
6 jiggers creme de cacao or kahlua

4 jiggers carrot juice or purée
Cinnamon sticks

Blend sweet cream with creme de cacao or kahlua and carrot juice or purée. Pour the mixture into chilled liqueur glasses and serve with cinnamon stick swizzle in each.

ORANGE LADY

PREPARATION: 5-10 MINUTES   **SERVES: TWO**

½ jigger grenadine syrup
4 jiggers orange juice concentrate, undiluted
4 jiggers vodka

4 jiggers carrot juice or purée
Crushed ice

Mix all ingredients together thoroughly and serve over crushed ice.

CARROT COOLER

PREPARATION: 5-10 MINUTES   **SERVES: TWO**

⅔ cup carrot juice or purée
⅔ cup dry white wine
⅔ cup apricot nectar

Dash grenadine syrup
Crushed ice
Lemon twists

Blend the carrot juice or purée, white wine and apricot nectar. Stir in the grenadine syrup and pour the mixture over crushed ice in two tall frosted glasses. Garnish each with a twist of lemon.

SOUPS!

C H A P T E R   6

A SOUP FOR ALL SEASONS

PREPARATION: 25-30 MINUTES   **SERVES: 4-6**

Carrot experts tell us that the beta-carotene content of this remarkable vegetable doesn't go down during storage — it goes up. You don't have to stop using carrots when their growing season is past to catch them at their best... which means you can enjoy soups like this all year round.

3 cups sliced carrots
1 small onion, chopped
1 leek, chopped
2 stalks celery, sliced
4-5 cups chicken broth

⅓ cup rice, uncooked
Salt and pepper to taste
¾ cup light cream
Chopped dill or parsley

Place the carrots, onion, leek, and celery in a large saucepan with 4 cups of chicken broth and the rice.

Bring to a boil, cover the pan, and reduce the heat, cooking gently for 15–20 minutes or until the vegetables are tender.

Purée in a blender, vegetable mill, or food pro- cessor. Return to the saucepan and add an additional cup of chicken broth if the soup is too thick.

Season to taste with salt and pepper, add the light cream, and reheat to just under the boiling point.

Sprinkle the soup with chopped dill or parsley and serve at once.

A DILLY OF A CARROT SOUP

PREPARATION: 20-25 MINUTES   **COOLING: 2 HOURS**   **SERVES: 4-6**

The warm color of carrots and the cool taste of dill blend subtly in a soup that will delight the palates at your table. It's served cold, so you may want to reserve it for warm weather meals. (Read on for hot carrot soups!)

3 cups carrot coins
¼ cup diced onion
½ celery stalk, diced
⅛ teaspoon dill seed

3 cups chicken stock
Salt and pepper to taste
½ cup plain yogurt
¼ cup chives, chopped

Cook the carrots, onions, celery and dill seed in chicken stock in a medium saucepan until the vegetables are tender. Cool.

Purée the carrot mixture and correct the seasonings, adding salt and pepper to taste.

Pour the mixture into a covered glass or plastic container and chill in the refrigerator for at least two hours before serving.

Spoon a twist of yogurt onto each individual cup or bowl, and sprinkle with chives as you serve it.

CARROT SOUP

PREPARATION: 20-25 MINUTES   **SERVES: 4-6**

We thought of this as "plain" Carrot Soup at first. Upon reflection, however, we feel we should call this "fancy" Carrot Soup.

2 cups diced carrots
1½ cups diced potatoes
¼ cup diced onion
3-4 cups water

2 slices bacon
½ cup soft bread crumbs
2 tablespoons butter or margarine
Salt and pepper to taste

Combine the carrots, potatoes, onion, and three of the four cups of water in a medium saucepan, cover, and cook until the vegetables are tender.

While the vegetables are cooking, fry the bacon until it is crisp, crumble it, and set it aside.

When the vegetables are tender, stir in the soft bread crumbs and the butter or margarine, and season the soup with salt and pepper to taste.

If you think it needs it, add the remaining cup of water to the broth, bring it back to the boiling point, and simmer for 5 minutes or so.

At serving time sprinkle the bacon over each bowl, or add it to the tureen just before you place it on the table.

KING MIDAS CARROT SOUP

PREPARATION: 20-25 MINUTES   **SERVES: 4-6**

It's our bet that if King Midas had gotten all the carrot soup he wanted, he wouldn't have been so greedy when it came to gold!

4 carrots, diced
2 potatoes, chopped
2 celery stalks, chopped
1 onion, chopped
3 cups chicken stock

Salt and pepper to taste
Pinch of dill seed
1 cup water
⅓ cup dry milk solids
3 tablespoons butter or margarine

Place the diced carrots, potatoes, celery and onions in a large covered saucepan with the chicken stock.

Add the salt and pepper to taste, along with the dill seed. Simmer, covered, until the vegetables are tender. Remove from the heat, cool as necessary, and purée. Return to the saucepan and reheat, adding the water, dry milk solids, and butter or margarine.

Serve piping hot.

CREAM OF CARROT SOUP

Guests tend to go wild over this soup. We say there's nothing to it, that it's only a simple little soup. They tell us the ability to make a good soup is the mark of a good cook.

2 tablespoons butter or margarine
½ cup minced onion
1 tablespoon flour
3½ cups chicken stock
1½ cups carrot coins

1½ cups diced potatoes
Dash rosemary
Salt and pepper to taste
½ cup plain yogurt
2 tablespoons minced parsley

Melt the butter in a medium saucepan and sauté the onions until they are soft and translucent. Blend in the flour.

Gradually stir in the chicken stock and all the remaining ingredients except for the yogurt and the parsley.

Simmer until the vegetables are tender, remove from the heat and allow the pan to cool slightly. Purée the carrot mixture, return it to the saucepan, and bring it to just under a boil. Correct the seasoning.

Fold in the yogurt, reheat, and serve at once, sprinkling each serving with a little parsley.

CREAM OF CARROT SOUP JR.

Every cook worthy of the name seems to have a favorite cream soup recipe. This one came our way from a friend who thought it very similar to our Cream of Carrot Soup above. They are similar, but this one doesn't include potatoes and some of the directions are different. Both are terrific.

2 cups diced carrots
1 cup water
1 tablespoon minced onion
3 tablespoons melted butter or margarine

3 tablespoons flour
2½ cups milk
Salt and pepper

Combine the carrots and the water, cover and simmer until the carrots are tender. Rub the carrots through a sieve, purée them in a blender, or process them until smooth.

Brown the onions in the butter or margarine, add the flour, and mix until smooth.

Add the milk slowly and cook until thick, stirring constantly to keep the mixture from forming lumps.

Add the carrots and the water in which they were cooked, blending thoroughly.

Season to taste, heat through and serve at once.

POTAGE CRÉCY

PREPARATION: 20-25 MINUTES   **SERVES: 4-6**

2 tablespoons butter or margarine
¾ cup diced onion
3 cups grated carrots
4 cups chicken stock
1 8-ounce can tomato sauce

2 tablespoons rice or rosarina pasta
Salt and pepper to taste
½ cup light cream
4 tablespoons butter or margarine

Melt the two tablespoons of butter or margarine in a large saucepan. Add the onions and sauté until translucent.

Stir in the carrots, the stock, the tomato sauce, and the rice or rosarina and simmer until the carrots are tender.

Remove from the heat, cool as necessary, and purée.

Return the carrot mixture to the saucepan, reheat, season with salt and pepper to taste, and add the cream.

Just before serving, stir in the four tablespoons of butter or margarine. (Butter is a good complement for beta-carotene-rich carrots.)

RICH-AS-CROESUS SOUP

PREPARATION: 20-25 MINUTES   **SERVES: 4-6**

It may be stretching a point to imply that you'll become as rich as Croesus if you find a bowl of this carrot soup at your place. But when you eat it you'll certainly feel like a million.

2 tablespoons butter or margarine
1 small onion, diced
3 cups carrots, diced
¼ cup quick-cooking rice

3 cups chicken stock
1 cup milk
1 teaspoon sugar
Salt and pepper to taste

Melt the butter or margarine in a large covered pot, add the onion and carrots, cover, and cook until the onions are translucent.

Add the rice and the chicken stock. Cover and cook until the rice is tender, about 10 minutes.

Remove from the heat, cool as necessary, and blend the mixture until it is smooth.

Return to the cooking pot and add the milk and sugar. Reheat to just under the boiling point.

Season to taste with salt and pepper, and serve hot.

POT OF GOLD SOUP

PREPARATION: 20-25 MINUTES   **SERVES: 4-6**

It's difficult to describe to someone who's never thought of carrots as the basis for gourmet soups, just how elegant a tureen of this creamy golden mixture can be. But there's one sure way to test what we say: try some for yourself.

3 cups diced carrots
2½ cups diced potatoes
3½ cups water
Pinch nutmeg

Salt and pepper to taste
2 cups milk
2 tablespoons butter or margarine
Chopped parsley

Bring the carrots and the potatoes to a boil in the water in a large, covered pot. Add the nutmeg, salt and pepper to taste, and cook, covered, until the vegetables are very tender.

Remove from the heat, cool as necessary, and purée the carrot mixture.

Return the mixture to the cooking pot, add the milk and reheat to the boiling point.

Correct the seasonings, remove from the heat, and add the butter or margarine and a sprinkle of parsley just as you serve.

CARROT PURÉE

PREPARATION: 15-25 MINUTES   **SERVES: 4-6**

Carrots are colorful by nature... bold, bright, self-assured. There is nothing pale or peaked about carrots. You can count on them to be themselves, even after you have removed their tops, peeled or scraped them, cut them up in pieces, boiled them in water, and ground them to bits. After going through all that, they will still be orange, still be flavorful, still be carrots.

6 medium carrots
3 cups water
1 tablespoon butter or margarine
1 tablespoon flour
2 cups liquid from carrots

3 tablespoons dry milk solids
Salt and pepper to taste
1 tablespoon finely grated orange rind
Parsley or mint, minced

Cook the carrots in the three cups of water until tender. Drain, reserving the liquid. Purée the carrot solids.

Meanwhile melt the butter or margarine in another saucepan, add the flour, and stir to mix well. When the mixture is bubbling, add two cups of the reserved carrot liquid, the dry milk solids, the salt and pepper to taste, and the orange rind. Stir in the puréed carrot solids.

Stir over a low heat until all the flavors are well blended and the mixture is hot but not boiling.

Dust with mint or parsley and serve at once.

CRÉCYSSOISE

The name of this best-of-its-kind carrot soup means, literally, a female resident of Crecy *(the region of France where most of that country's carrots are grown), just as "Vichyssoise" means* a female resident of Vichy. *Though our* Crécyssoise *is usually served well-chilled, it tastes good hot, too.*

2 cups sliced carrots
¼ cup chopped celery
½ medium onion, chopped
Salt to taste
2 peppercorns
½ bay leaf
1½ cups chicken broth

2 tablespoons butter or margarine
⅛ cup flour
2 cups milk
Dash cayenne
Dash nutmeg
Parsley, chopped

Cook the carrots, celery, onion, salt, peppercorns, and bay leaf in the chicken broth. Simmer until the vegetables are tender.

Remove the bay leaf and the peppercorns, cool as necessary, and purée the mixture in a blender or processor.

Meanwhile, in another saucepan, melt the butter or margarine, stir in the flour, and make a white sauce with the milk, whisking and stirring to prevent sticking and lumping.

Add the cayenne pepper, nutmeg, and carrot purée, blending all ingredients thoroughly.

Turn into a glass or plastic container and chill for at least two hours.

Serve very cold, with a sprinkle of chopped parsley on each serving.

CARROT, CLAM AND CORN CHOWDER

PREPARATION: 30-45 MINUTES   **SERVES: 4-8**

Colorful carrots turn what would otherwise be an ordinary-looking soup into a bright, rich and tasty main-course dish. You may want to double these amounts the second time you make it. It's almost better warmed over than it is the first time.

(Serve a loaf of hot, crusty bread and a crisp, tossed, green salad with this soup. A perfect meal.)

4 tablespoons butter or margarine
½ cup diced onion
½ cup diced celery
3 tablespoons flour
3-5 cups chicken stock
½ cup dry milk solids
1 16-ounce can whole corn
with liquid

3 cups diced carrots
3 cups diced potatoes
⅛ teaspoon cumin
⅛ teaspoon sage
⅛ teaspoon rosemary
2 6½-ounce cans chopped clams
Salt and pepper to taste

Melt the butter or margarine in a large saucepan and sauté the onions and celery until soft. Remove the vegetables and set aside, then stir the flour into the remaining butter or margarine and make a smooth thick paste.

Stir in three cups of the stock and the dry milk solids. Add the cooked onions and celery to the pot, along with the corn, the carrots, potatoes, spices and chopped clams, including the clam juice. Salt and pepper to taste.

Cover the pot and simmer for 15–20 minutes, stirring occasionally to keep things from sticking and burning. Add more of the remaining stock if it seems to be getting too thick.

Correct the seasonings if necessary and keep it just below a simmer for 15 minutes more. (The few minutes extra are worth it.)

Serve piping hot in large soup bowls or plates. Be prepared to whip off your apron and take bows.

CARROT COIN SOUP

2 tablespoons butter or margarine
1 onion, diced
2 tablespoons flour
4 cups chicken stock
3 cups carrot coins
2 cups diced potatoes

2 tablespoons minced parsley
Pinch of paprika
Dash of cumin and rosemary
Pinch of celery seed
Salt and pepper to taste
1 cup plain yogurt (optional)

In a large saucepan melt the butter or margarine, stir in the onion, and cook until soft.

Add the flour and stir until well blended. Gradually add the chicken stock, stirring constantly to keep the mixture from forming lumps.

Add the carrots, potatoes, parsley, paprika, cumin, rosemary, and celery seed.

Simmer until the vegetables are tender. Add salt and pepper to taste.

(Stir in the yogurt, if you like, just before you are ready to serve.)

CLAN MAC CARROT BROTH

1 pound lean lamb, cubed
3 tablespoons flour
4-6 cups water
1 tablespoon lemon juice
½ cup barley
⅛ teaspoon cumin
¼ teaspoon rosemary

4 large carrots, cubed
1 onion, diced
2 potatoes, cubed
2 stalks celery, diced
Salt and pepper to taste
1 15-ounce can kidney beans
1 bay leaf

Brown the meat in a large pot, sprinkle the flour over it, and stir until the pieces are well coated and the flour is brown. Stir in four cups of the water, blending until a smooth thin sauce has formed. Hold the remaining two cups of water in reserve for later use if needed.

Add all the other ingredients, including the liquid from the kidney beans. Cover the pot and simmer for at least one hour, stirring occasionally.

If the broth becomes too thick, add some of the reserved water.

When all is ready, remove bay leaf and serve piping hot to cheers from the clan.

GOLDEN STATE SOUP

PREPARATION: 25-30 MINUTES   **SERVES: 4-6**

In late spring and summer California is literally the Golden State. Its hills and mountains are covered with dry yellow grass and tawny shrubs. And, since California is where most of our golden carrots are grown, we thought it appropriate to name this soup after it.

Like many soups, this one seems to taste even better as a leftover, making it ideal for ahead-of-time preparation.

4 tablespoons butter or margarine
1 tablespoon flour
½ cup minced onion
1 cup diced celery
3 cups diced carrots

1½ cups diced potatoes
3 cups beef broth
Salt and pepper to taste
Dash of nutmeg

Heat the butter or margarine in a large saucepan. Stir in the flour and mix into a smooth paste, then add the onion, celery, carrots and potatoes, covering them with the broth.

Simmer until all the vegetables are tender, but not mushy, correct the seasonings with salt and pepper to taste, and sprinkle a dash of nutmeg on each serving as you ladle it out.

ONE-DAY SOUP

Remember the children's nursery rhyme about soup? "Some like it hot/ Some like it cold/ Some like it in the pot/ Nine days old." It must *have been written about this one. But those who "like it in the pot, nine days old," will be out of luck: it will be gone long before then.*

3 cups diced carrots
¼ cup diced onion
1 stalk celery, diced
2¾ cups chicken stock
1½ tablespoons flour

¼ cup water
Salt and pepper to taste
½ cup sour cream or plain yogurt
¼ cup minced parsley
Pinch cayenne pepper

In a large covered saucepan, simmer the carrots, onion and celery in the chicken stock until they are tender. Remove the pan from the heat and add the cayenne pepper. Let the mixture cool slightly.

While it's cooling, mix the flour and the quarter of a cup of water together into a smooth paste. Set this aside.

Now, purée the carrot mixture, return it to the saucepan and heat it gently until just under boiling.

Add the thickening paste a little at a time, making sure you don't thicken the soup too much. Whisk and stir to remove any lumps that may have formed.

Check the seasonings and add salt and pepper to taste.

Just before you are ready to sit down to eat, fold in the sour cream or yogurt. Pour into a serving tureen or individual bowls, sprinkle with parsley, and serve.

SALADS

CHAPTER 7

CARROT CRUNCH SALAD

PREPARATION: 10-15 MINUTES   **SERVES: 4-6**

The carrot/mayonnaise/yogurt mixture can be prepared ahead of time, covered, and stored in the refrigerator. Add the nuts and parsley just before serving.

2 cups grated carrots
3 tablespoons mayonnaise
3 tablespoons pineapple yogurt

¼ cup chopped nuts
2 tablespoons chopped parsley
Salad greens

Thoroughly mix the carrots, mayonnaise and yogurt in a medium bowl.

Fold in the nuts and parsley and serve on a bed of crisp salad greens.

COLUMBUS DAY CARROT SALAD

PREPARATION: 10-15 MINUTES   **CHILLING: 2-3 HOURS**   **SERVES: 4-6**

This zesty dish is nutritious enough to serve as a main course. It would be good with Cheery Carroty Corn Bread *(p. 119), followed by a plate of* Carroty Chocolate Bars *(p. 133) for dessert.*

3 tablespoons Italian dressing
¾ cup mild cheese, cubed
¾ cup thin carrot coins
¼ cup diced green pepper

½ cup zucchini, peeled and cut in 1-inch strips
Oregano to taste
1 15½-ounce can red kidney beans, drained
Salad greens

Combine the dressing, cheese, vegetables and oregano in a mixing bowl, and blend well.
Carefully fold in the kidney beans.

Let the mixture stand, covered, in the refrigerator for two or three hours, to allow the flavors to blend, and then serve on crisp salad greens.

SERENDIPITY SALAD

PREPARATION: 5-10 MINUTES   **CHILLING: 1 HOUR**   **SERVES: 4-6**

This has always been one of our favorite carrot salads. The textures of carrot and raisin are so different that they are most interesting when put together. The dish looks good, too: bright orange carrots set off by dark raisins, all on a green background. The lemon-flavored yogurt is a tasty serendipity.

4 tablespoons mayonnaise
¼ cup lemon-flavored yogurt
Salt to taste

2 cups finely grated carrots
¾ cup raisins
Salad greens

In a medium mixing bowl combine the mayonnaise, yogurt, and salt, and blend well.

Stir in the carrots and raisins, mixing thoroughly.

Cover and chill for at least an hour before serving on crisp salad greens.

KING CARROT SALAD

PREPARATION: 10-15 MINUTES   **SERVES: 4**

1 tablespoon lemon juice
¼ cup vegetable oil
Salt and pepper to taste
4 carrots, grated

1 green onion, chopped
Salad greens
Chopped parsley

Combine the lemon juice, oil, salt and pepper in a medium bowl and whisk until light and frothy.

Add the carrots and onion and toss to cover with the lemon juice mixture.

Arrange the salad on crisp salad greens and sprinkle with chopped parsley. Serve at once.

TRI-COLOR SALAD

PREPARATION: 10-15 MINUTES   **SERVES: 4-6**

Bright green peas, orange carrots, and deep green broccoli team up in this simple, delicious salad. With the exception of the salad greens, the vegetables are cooked to make the most of the beta-carotene they all contain. Save the drained liquids from the carrots, peas and broccoli for use in a soup or broth.

1 cup cooked carrots, diced
1 cup cooked broccoli pieces
1 cup cooked peas

Roquefort dressing
Salt and pepper to taste
Salad greens

Combine the carrots, broccoli and peas with the dressing and seasonings, tossing to mix. Be careful not to crush the vegetables.

Arrange the salad mixture on crisp greens and serve at once.

SALADE CITRONNÉE

PREPARATION: 10-15 MINUTES   **CHILLING: 2-3 HOURS**   **SERVES: 6-8**

3 ounces lemon gelatin
¼ cup sugar
1½ cups boiling water
4 ounces cream cheese
¼ cup lemonade

½ teaspoon grated lemon peel
1 tablespoon lemon juice
1 cup grated carrots
1 cup grated apple
Twists of lemon

Dissolve the gelatin and sugar in boiling water. Set aside.

When the gelatin mixture is cool, add the softened cream cheese and beat until smooth. Stir in the lemonade, lemon peel, and lemon juice.

Chill the mixture until it is partially set. Add the carrots and apple.

Spoon the mixture into six to eight individual molds and chill until firm. Unmold and garnish with twists of lemon.

PENELOPE'S FAVORITE PICNIC SALAD

PREPARATION: 5-15 MINUTES   **SERVES: 4-6**

Is this salad the real reason that Odysseus persevered and finally made it home to Ithaka 20 years after leaving to fight the Trojan War? Homer doesn't say that's why the wily fighter gave up sirens and goddesses, but....

1 cup pitted green olives
3 celery stalks, diced
3 green onions, diced
2 cups grated carrots

Salt and pepper to taste
2 tablespoons vegetable oil
2 tablespoons wine vinegar
Salad greens

In a large bowl combine the olives, celery, onions, and carrots. Set aside.

Combine the salt and pepper, oil, and vinegar and whisk until frothy and cloudy.

Pour the oil and vinegar mixture over the carrot mixture, toss to coat, and serve on crisp salad greens.

CARROT AND PEAR SALAD

PREPARATION: 10-15 MINUTES   **SERVES: 4**

Orange carrots bursting with beta-carotene combine with white pear halves, warm brown cinnamon flavor and cool white yogurt to make as pretty a salad as you'll ever want to see.

Raisins may be sprinkled on top, if desired, for garnish.

2 cups cooked carrot coins
¼ cup plain yogurt
⅛ teaspoon cinnamon
4 fresh pear halves or

4 canned pear halves, drained
Lemon juice
Raisins (optional)

Put the carrots into the refrigerator to chill while you blend the yogurt and cinnamon in a small bowl and set aside.

Prepare the fresh pears and sprinkle them with the lemon juice to keep them white; or, drain the canned pear halves. Arrange the pears on crisp lettuce leaves.

Divide the carrots evenly and arrange them in center of each pear half, either in a mound or in domino rows.

Pour the yogurt mixture over the carrots and pears and serve at once.

MIX AND MATCH MOLDED SALAD

PREPARATION: 10-15 MINUTES

YIELD: ONE 1-QUART MOLD, OR 6 SERVINGS

CHILLING: 2-3 HOURS

The carrots are crunchy, the gelatin smooth, the orange sweet, the coconut mild. They blend together well in this fix-ahead-of-time gelatin-based salad.

3 ounces orange-flavored gelatin
1½ cups boiling water
1 cup crushed orange pulp

2 cups grated carrots
½ cup flaked coconut
¼ cup chopped nuts (optional)

In a medium mixing bowl, dissolve the gelatin in the boiling water. Set aside.

Drain the crushed orange pulp, reserving the juice, and set aside.

Add the orange juice to the gelatin and chill until the mixture is the consistency of unbeaten egg white.

Stir in the reserved orange pulp, carrots, coconut and nuts. Pour into a lightly oiled one-quart mold, or six individual molds.

Chill the mixture until it is firm. Unmold on a bed of greens and serve at once.

ONE FOR THE MONEY SLAW

PREPARATION: 15-20 MINUTES   **CHILLING: 1-2 HOURS**   **SERVES: 4-6**

1. Carrots are the champions of Beta-carotene.
2. Cabbage is one of the cruciferous vegetables.

3. Oranges are rich in vitamin C.
4. Get ready. Get set. Go!

½ cup mayonnaise
1 tablespoon sugar
2 tablespoons lemon juice
1 teaspoon salt or to taste

Pepper to taste
4 cups shredded cabbage
2 cups shredded carrots
1 cup orange sections

In a large bowl blend together the mayonnaise, sugar, lemon juice, salt and pepper.
Add the cabbage, carrots and orange sections.

Mix well.
Cover and refrigerate for one to two hours before serving.

HALLOWEEN SALAD

PREPARATION: 10-15 MINUTES   **CHILLING: 1 HOUR**   **SERVES: 4-6**

Orange and black are the traditional colors of Halloween. This salad will be perfect for that occasion, with its true orange carrots and jet black olives. (Offering such a treat to the right ghosts and goblins could save you from a trick or two!)

4 medium large carrots
1 tablespoon green onion pieces
1 tablespoon chopped parsley

Pinch of dill seed
½ cup sliced black olives
Oil and vinegar dressing

Grate the carrots coarsely and toss with the other ingredients in a large bowl with the oil and vinegar dressing.

Cover and chill for at least an hour before serving.

THREE'S COMPANY SLAW

The recipe that follows calls for three ingredients that look good, taste good, and are good for you. Despite their differences, they go together well.

2 apples, cored and diced
Dash lemon juice
1 cup finely grated carrots
1 cup finely chopped cabbage
¼ cup mayonnaise

¼ cup plain yogurt
1 teaspoon sugar
Dash salt, or to taste
Dash nutmeg
Shredded lettuce

Sprinkle the apples with the lemon juice, then toss with the carrots and cabbage in a mixing bowl. Set this aside.

In a smaller mixing bowl, blend the mayonnaise, yogurt, sugar, salt and nutmeg well, then pour this mixture over the carrot mixture.

Toss carefully but well, and then cover and chill for at least an hour before serving, to give the flavors plenty of time to get together.

Serve on a bed of shredded lettuce.

CARROTS, BEANS, AND GREENS SALAD

PREPARATION: 10-15 MINUTES   **CHILLING: 1-2 HOURS**   **SERVES: 4**

This substantial salad can serve as your main course, accompanied by crusty hard rolls and butter — perhaps preceded by bowls of good, nourishing Carrot, Clam and Corn Chowder *(p. 45)*

1 cup grated carrots
¼ cup chopped green pepper
½ cup diced celery
1 tablespoon chopped onion
Salt and pepper to taste

1 15¼-ounce can pork and beans
½ cup shoestring-size cheese strips
½ cup diced apple, unpeeled
Lettuce leaves

Combine all the ingredients in a medium mixing bowl, tossing carefully to avoid mashing the beans.

Cover the bowl and refrigerate it for a couple of hours to allow the flavors to blend.

Serve the salad on a bed of lettuce on a platter or plate, or on individual salad plates.

PLAIN JANE CARROT SALAD

PREPARATION: 5-10 MINUTES   **CHILLING: 1 HOUR**   **SERVES: 4**

4 medium carrots
2 tablespoons wine vinegar
2 tablespoons vegetable oil

Salt and pepper to taste
Lettuce leaves

Wash and peel the carrots and shred or grate them into a medium serving bowl.

Combine the vinegar, oil, salt and pepper, pour over the carrots, and toss the mixture lightly.

Chill for at least an hour. Serve on lettuce leaves.

GOLD SOVEREIGN SALAD

PREPARATION: 5-10 MINUTES **SERVES: 4**

2 cups cooked carrot coins
1 cup cooked broccoli pieces
2 stalks celery, diced, raw
Salt and pepper to taste

4 tablespoons lemon-flavored yogurt
¼ cup mayonnaise
Salad greens

Mix the carrots, broccoli, celery and seasonings with a dressing made by combining the yogurt and the mayonnaise.

Toss all the ingredients together, being careful not to crush the carrots and the broccoli.

Store the mixture, covered, in the refrigerator until it is well chilled. Serve on a bed of crisp salad greens.

OKTOBERSALAD

PREPARATION: 10-15 MINUTES **SERVES: 4**

Red-cheeked apples and orange carrots remind us of autumn's bright beauty. Serve this colorful salad with one of the many main dish recipes that start on p. 61, accompanied by hot rolls and butter or margarine.

2 large carrots, grated
2 large apples, shredded
1 tablespoon lemon juice

2 tablespoons vegetable oil
Salt and pepper to taste
Salad greens

Place the grated carrots and the apples in a large salad bowl and toss to mix them thoroughly.

In another bowl, whisk or beat the lemon juice, oil, salt, and pepper together until they are well blended.

Pour the oil mixture over the carrots and apples, toss to coat them, and serve at once on salad greens.

WHITE-ON-WHITE SALAD

Here's a tart, tangy, tasty salad easy to whip up and certain to please. Crunchy orange carrots contrast with pale soft pears and stark white chewy cheese curds, all blended together with tangy yellow lemon juice and topped by a dash of perky brown nutmeg.

2 large carrots, grated
1 cup large curd cottage cheese
1 tablespoon lemon juice

1 medium can pears, drained
Salad greens
Dash nutmeg

In a mixing bowl, combine the carrots, cottage cheese and lemon juice. Set aside.

Cut the well-drained pears into quarters and then into eighths, being careful not to crush them. (Reserve the juice for a breakfast drink.)

Add the pear pieces to the carrot mixture and toss carefully to blend. Arrange the mixture on the salad greens and serve at once, sprinkling each serving with a dash of nutmeg.

MAIN DISHES

CHAPTER 8

QUICHE CRÉCY

1 9-inch unbaked pie crust
1¾ cups milk, scalded
1 tablespoon butter or margarine
1 small onion, diced
3 eggs

Salt and pepper to taste
½ cup cooked diced broccoli
1½ cups cooked diced carrots
½ cup diced cheese

Preheat oven to 400°F.

Have the pie crust ready in your refrigerator. Scald the milk and set it aside to cool. Meanwhile, melt the butter or margarine in a small frying pan and sauté the onion until it is translucent and soft. Set it aside. Mix together the eggs and the partially cooled scalded milk, salt and pepper. Beat together well.

Get out the pie crust and distribute the broccoli, carrots, cheese and onion in it. Pour the egg mixture over all. Bake the quiche 30–45 minutes, or until a kitchen knife inserted in the center comes out clean.

Remove it from the oven and let it stand for 10 minutes before serving.

(If you want to cut down on your calories, but not on your quiche, make it without the pie crust in a buttered pie plate.)

BLUE-RIBBON VEGETABLE PIE

PREPARATION: 35-40 MINUTES　　　**BAKING: 25-30 MINUTES**　　　**SERVES: 6**

Get ready for raves — maybe even awards — when you serve this crusty, tasty carroty vegetable pie. The work it takes is worth it. Beta-carotene is always worth it.

Pastry for one 9-inch pie crust
1 cup carrots, coined
1 cup broccoli pieces
1 cup peas, fresh or frozen
½ pound mushrooms
1 small onion, diced
3 tablespoons butter or margarine

3 tablespoons flour
¼ cup minced parsley
Salt and pepper to taste
½ cup beef broth
Milk (about 1 cup)
½ cup sliced water chestnuts

Preheat oven to 400°F.

Have ready to hand enough pastry for a one-crust 9-inch pie. Keep it covered tightly and in the refrigerator until you are ready to roll it out.

While it is chilling, cook the carrots, broccoli and peas separately, reserving the cooking liquid from each. Combine the vegetables with the mushrooms in a large bowl and set this aside.

Sauté the onion in butter or margarine until it is translucent, and then stir in the flour, parsley, salt and pepper. Mix until the sauce is smooth and then add the beef broth and the milk combined with the reserved vegetable liquids to make 1½ cups.

Cook, stirring constantly, until the sauce is the consistency of a medium white sauce — that is, neither too thick nor too thin. If it gets too thick, add some more of the reserved liquids or milk.

Remove from the heat, stir in the vegetables, the mushrooms and the drained water chestnuts, and turn into a buttered 2½–3-quart casserole.

Retrieve the pastry from the refrigerator, roll it out to fit over the top of the casserole, seal the edges, and prick the top to allow the steam to escape.

Now, carefully and tenderly — mindful of how much time this work of art has consumed already — slide the casserole into the pre-heated oven. Allow it to bake for some 25–30 minutes, or until the pastry is a golden brown, the sauce is bubbling up through the openings in the top, and the whole delicious *chef d'oeuvre* is ready to set before family, friends or... judges?

TENDER LOVING LASAGNA

Just plain lasagna is one of our favorite dishes, but Tender Loving Lasagna *is especially good since it is made with two full cups of beta-carotene-rich carrots. With those credentials it's a dish you can't refuse.*

2 cups diced tomatoes
2 8-ounce cans tomato sauce
1 teaspoon oregano
½ cup minced onion
1 small clove garlic, minced
4 tablespoons olive oil
¾ pound lean ground beef

2 cups cooked carrot coins
Salt and pepper to taste
8 ounces lasagna noodles
12 ounces dry curd cottage cheese
2 cups grated Mozzarella cheese
½ cup grated Parmesan cheese

Preheat oven to 350°F.

Combine the diced tomatoes, tomato sauce and oregano in a medium-large saucepan and start them simmering, uncovered. Heat the olive oil in a medium frying pan, and sauté the onion and garlic until the onion is soft and translucent. Stir in the ground beef and cook it until it is brown.

Drain off all the fat and add the meat mixture to the tomato sauce. Stir in the carrots, add salt and pepper to taste and simmer the mixture for 1–2 hours.

Meanwhile, prepare the lasagna noodles according to the package directions, drain them and set them aside.

Cover the bottom of a 9" x 13" baking dish with about a quarter of the sauce mixture. Arrange a layer of the lasagna noodles in parallel strips over the sauce. On top of the noodles spread a third of the cottage cheese with a third of the Mozzarella cheese on top of that.

Repeat the layers, beginning again with the sauce. You should have enough of everything to repeat the layers again, or three times altogether.

Save enough of the sauce to make it the last, or top, layer. Sprinkle over it the grated Parmesan cheese.

Bake the lasagna in a pre-heated oven for 30 minutes, remove and let it stand for 10 minutes before you cut it into squares for serving.

FETTUCINI CARROTINI

2 tablespoons butter or margarine
¼ cup minced onion
½ cup minced celery
1 cup grated carrots
2 cups tomato pieces
1 16-ounce can tomato sauce
¼ teaspoon oregano
¼ teaspoon minced garlic

1 teaspoon sugar
Salt and pepper to taste
8 cups water
Salt to taste
8 ounces fettucini noodles
6 tablespoons butter or margarine
¼ cup minced parsley
½ cup grated sharp cheese

In a medium saucepan melt the 2 tablespoons of butter or margarine and sauté the onions, celery and carrots until they are soft. Stir in the tomato pieces, tomato sauce, oregano and garlic. Blend them well and bring them to a boil. Add the sugar, and salt and pepper to taste.

Reduce the heat, cover the pan and simmer, stirring occasionally, for at least 30 minutes. If the sauce gets too thick, add a little water.

Meanwhile, get the pasta ready by bringing the eight cups of water to boil in a large saucepan, add salt or to your taste, and prepare the noodles according to package directions.

When the noodles are at the *al dente* stage drain them well, return them to the pan, and toss them gently with the 6 tablespoons of butter or margarine and the parsley, making sure all are coated. If you have to keep them warm for a few minutes while you wait for the sauce, set the saucepan in a larger container with a little hot water in it and set it on low heat.

When the sauce is ready, turn the noodles out into a serving dish, spoon the sauce over the top and sprinkle with grated cheese. Serve at once.

MACARONI CON CARROTS

PREPARATION: 15 MINUTES   **BAKING: 30-45 MINUTES**   **SERVES: 4-8**

This is one of our all-time favorites and it proves once again that recipes don't have to be complicated to be good. Basically, it's just good old everyday macaroni and cheese — with one big difference: Carrots... best ever for beta-carotene.

3 quarts water
8 ounces macaroni
1 small onion, minced
1½ cups grated carrots
1 teaspoon salt, or to taste
4 tablespoons butter or margarine

4 tablespoons flour
4 cups milk
1½ cups grated cheese
Salt and pepper to taste
1 cup crumbled potato chips

Preheat oven to 375°F.

Bring the water to a boil in a large saucepan, add the macaroni, onion, carrots, and salt, and cook until the macaroni is tender, about 10 minutes. Drain the mixture and turn it into a 3-quart casserole or other good-sized baking dish. Set this aside.

In another saucepan melt the butter or margarine and stir in the flour to make a smooth paste. Gradually stir in the milk and bring it to a boil over a medium heat, stirring it constantly to keep it from forming lumps. Add the cheese and the salt and pepper to taste. Stir until the cheese is melted. Pour the sauce over the macaroni, sprinkle with the crumbled potato chips, and bake, uncovered, for 30–45 minutes.

CONFETTI OMELETTI

PREPARATION: 10-15 MINUTES   **BAKING: 30-35 MINUTES**   **SERVES: 4-8**

Serve this omelet just once, and we guarantee that whoever shares it with you will insist on having it again and again. It's delicious, it's colorful, it's nutritious... and with just a hint of a foreign accent.

4 eggs
⅔ cup milk
¼ cup flour
2 tablespoons wheat germ
1½ cups grated carrots

1½ cups grated Italian squash
2 tablespoons diced scallions
¼ cup minced parsley
1 cup shredded cheese
Salt and pepper to taste

Preheat oven to 375°F.

In a large mixing bowl heat the eggs, milk, flour, and wheat germ until smooth. Stir in the carrots, Italian squash, scallions, parsley, and shredded cheese, mixing well.

Salt and pepper to taste.

Allow the mixture to stand for a few minutes, and then stir thoroughly again. (It is going to look too thick for a proper omelet mixture, but resist the temptation to add more milk. Both the carrots and the squash are mainly water — which is released as they cook.)

Pour the mixture into an oiled 13" x 8" x 2" baking dish and put it into a pre-heated oven.

Bake for 30–35 minutes, or until a knife inserted in the center comes out clean. Cool for five minutes before serving.

CARROT SCRAMBLE

PREPARATION: 12-15 MINUTES   **SERVES: 2-4**

If ever a breakfast dish said: "Have a nice day!" this one does. (Try it for late-night suppers, too, and send everyone to bed with a smile!)

1 tablespoon vegetable oil
¼ cup minced onion
1 medium carrot, grated or chopped very fine

5 eggs
⅓ cup milk
Salt and pepper to taste

Heat the oil in a medium frying pan and sauté the onion and carrots until they are soft and tender.

Meanwhile, beat the eggs, milk, and seasonings together and add them to the carrot mixture in the frying pan.

Stir and scramble until the mixture is done as you like it, and then serve with toast, muffins, bagels or rolls.

CARROT NESTS AND SHIRRED EGGS

PREPARATION: 15 MINUTES   **BAKING: 10-20 MINUTES**   **SERVES: 4**

This unusual arrangement of carrots, eggs and butter or margarine is almost guaranteed to make breakfast, brunch, or supper eaters sit up and take notice.

4 medium carrots
4-8 eggs
Salt and pepper to taste

4 pats butter or margarine
Sprinkle of parsley

Preheat oven to 350°F.

Slice the carrots into thin strips about 4 inches long, as if you were preparing potatoes for making french fries. Cook them in just enough water to keep them from burning, until they are at the crisp/tender stage.

When the carrots are ready, divide them evenly into four oiled individual oven-proof dishes. Break one or two eggs into each "nest." Season them to taste, and place a pat of butter or margarine on top.

Cover the dishes with lids or foil. Bake the nests until the egg whites are firm and the yolks are as you like them.

Remove the lids or foil, sprinkle with parsley, and serve at once.

CARROTS AND PEPPERS AND CHEESE

With protein from the cheese, vitamins and minerals and fiber from the vegetables, this is almost a one-dish meal. We add hard rolls and a salad to make it complete.

4 tablespoons butter or margarine
1 cup green pepper slices
½ cup diced green onions
2 cups grated carrots
¼ cup minced parsley
2 cups zucchini squash, cubed

Fresh dill (optional)
½ pound fresh mushrooms
Salt and pepper to taste
½ cup commercial sour cream
1 cup mild cheese, grated

Heat the butter or margarine in a medium covered saucepan and sauté the pepper and onion until soft. Add the carrots and cook for about five minutes.

Stir in the parsley, zucchini, dill, mushrooms, and salt and pepper to taste. Cover and cook until all the vegetables are tender.

(It's unlikely more liquid will be needed because the zucchini has so much water in it, but keep an eye on it just in case.)

When the vegetables are done, remove the pan from the heat, drain off the excess liquid, if any, and stir in the sour cream and cheese.

Give the cheese time to melt, then serve at once.

CARROTUNA CASSEROLE

The people at our house love this and wish we could have it at least once a week, year in and year out. It's wonderfully simple; it smells great while it's baking; it's almost a meal-in-one; and it's delicious warmed over.

1 8-ounce package macaroni
2 tablespoons butter or margarine
¼ cup minced onion
1 stalk celery, diced
2 tablespoons flour
1½ cups milk
1 9½-ounce can tuna, drained
2 cups grated carrots

1 cup buttermilk
1 cup dry curd cottage cheese
½ pound whole mushrooms
1 tablespoon soy sauce
Salt and pepper to taste
Dash garlic powder
1 cup grated cheese

Preheat oven to 350°F.

Cook the macaroni according to the package directions. Drain it and set it aside. While it's cooking, melt the butter or margarine in a medium pan and sauté the onion and celery until they are soft. Remove and set them aside.

Stir the flour into the butter or margarine and cook until it is bubbling. Blend in the milk to make a smooth light white sauce.

Remove the mixture from the heat. Add the tuna, carrots, buttermilk, cottage cheese, mushrooms, soy sauce, and other seasonings. Mix them together well. Stir in the onion and celery, then fold in the macaroni.

Pour this mixture into a buttered casserole dish, sprinkle the grated cheese over the top and bake it, covered, for 45 minutes. Remove the cover and bake for 15–20 minutes more, or until the cheese is melted and slightly crusty.

Serve at once.

ADRIENNE'S CLAMCARROT SPAGHETTI

A half pound of real *butter is used in this delectable, delicious — and probably sinful — recipe. We've tried it with only a quarter of a pound, and we've tried with margarine instead. But in this case, there's no substitute for the real thing.*

2 8-ounce cans chopped clams
½ pound whole mushrooms
2 16-ounce cans tomato sauce
1½ cups cooked puréed carrots
¼ cup minced onion
1 teaspoon ground basil
½-1 teaspoon garlic powder

¼ teaspoon crushed red pepper (optional)
½ cup minced parsley
Salt and pepper to taste
½ pound butter
Spaghetti
½ cup grated Romano cheese

Drain the clams, reserving the liquid. Add them with the mushrooms, to the tomato sauce, carrots and onions in a medium to large saucepan. Cook this mixture over medium heat, stirring occasionally. (Add some of the clam liquid if it gets too thick.)

Stir in the basil, garlic powder, (red pepper,) parsley, and salt and pepper to taste. Simmer for 15–20 minutes.

Finally, stir in the butter and keep the sauce just below the boiling point while you prepare the spaghetti according to the package directions.

When all is ready, spoon the sauce over the spaghetti, sprinkle with the grated cheese, and serve at once.

POULET CRÉCY au RIZ

PREPARATION: 20 MINUTES   **BAKING: 45–60 MINUTES**   **SERVES: 4-6**

4 chicken breast halves or thighs
2 tablespoons butter
1 small onion, minced
1 stalk celery, diced
2 cups chicken stock
2 cups tomato pieces
2 cups carrot coins

½ teaspoon rosemary
Dash garlic powder
¼ teaspoon oregano
Salt and pepper to taste
1 tablespoon minced parsley
1 cup raw rice

Preheat oven to 350°F.

Remove the skin and fat from the chicken pieces and sauté them in a medium frying pan until they are golden brown on both sides. Remove and set aside.

In the same pan sauté the onions and celery until the onions are translucent. Remove and set aside.

Into the same pan stir the chicken stock, tomatoes, carrot coins, rosemary, garlic powder, oregano, salt and pepper to taste, and parsley.

Add the rice to this mixture and stir everything together well. Pour into a 3-quart covered casserole.

Arrange the chicken pieces and reserved vegetables over the rice mixture, cover, and bake in a pre-heated oven for 45–60 minutes, or until the rice is done and the chicken is tender. Add a little water or tomato juice if it starts to look too dry during the baking.

Remove from the oven and serve at once.

COQ aux CAROTTES au VIN BLANC

PREPARATION: 20-25 MINUTES   **COOKING: 45-60 MINUTES**   **SERVES: 4**

2 tablespoons butter or margarine
½ cup chopped onion
4 chicken breast halves
Salt and pepper to taste
Garlic powder to taste
1 cup chicken stock
1 cup grated carrots

3 tablespoons minced parsley
⅛ teaspoon dill seed
⅛ teaspoon tarragon
⅛ teaspoon basil
⅛ teaspoon thyme
½ cup white wine

In a heavy skillet heat the butter or margarine and sauté the onion until it is tender. Remove the onion and set it aside.

Meanwhile, remove the fat and skin from the chicken pieces, sprinkle with the salt, pepper, and garlic powder, and then brown on both sides in the remaining butter or margarine. Remove the chicken and set aside.

Lower the heat under the skillet and stir in the cup of stock, the carrots, parsley, dill seed, tarragon, basil and thyme. Finally, add the white wine.

Now arrange the chicken pieces in the skillet, baste them with the wine mixture, cover tightly, and cook over low heat for 45-60 minutes.

Correct the seasonings, arrange the chicken on a serving plate, spoon the wine sauce over it, and it's ready to serve.

CARROT AND CHICKEN PILAF

PREPARATION: 20 MINUTES   **COOKING: 30-45 MINUTES**   **SERVES: 4**

4 chicken pieces
¼ pound butter or margarine
1½ cups rice, uncooked
1½ cups carrot coins
3 tablespoons minced parsley

¼ cup minced onion
3 cups chicken broth
½ pound fresh mushrooms
Dash cumin and rosemary
Salt and pepper to taste

Remove the skin and fat from the chicken pieces and brown them in the butter or margarine which has been heated in a medium-sized covered frying pan. Remove the chicken pieces and set aside.

Stir the rice into the butter or margarine remaining in the frying pan and stir it over medium to high heat until the rice is brown and looks slightly puffy and toasted. Reduce the heat to simmer, and add the carrot coins, parsley, onion, broth and mushrooms. Place the chicken pieces on top of the carrot/rice mixture, season with cumin, rosemary, and salt and pepper to taste. Cover the pan tightly and simmer until all the broth has been absorbed and the chicken and rice are tender.

Correct the seasonings and serve at once.

CARROT, CHICKEN AND ASPARAGUS

PREPARATION: 15 MINUTES　　　　　**BAKING: 45–60 MINUTES**　　　　　**SERVES: 4**

Different flavors, textures and colors get together under one cover here; each enhances the other.

2 tablespoons butter or margarine
2 tablespoons flour
2 cups milk
4 chicken breast halves or thighs
2 medium carrots, quartered
2 medium potatoes, quartered

8 asparagus spears, halved
1 bay leaf
2 peppercorns
1 tablespoon chopped parsley
2 tablespoons minced onion
Salt and pepper to taste

Preheat oven to 375°F.

Make a white sauce by melting the butter or margarine in a medium pan, and adding the flour to make a smooth paste. Blend in the milk and stir constantly until it is thickened. Remove from the heat and set aside.

Remove the skin and fat from the chicken. Arrange it with the vegetables in a covered casserole dish. Combine the white sauce with the bay leaf, peppercorns, parsley, and salt and pepper. Pour the sauce over the chicken and the vegetables in the casserole. Cover the casserole and bake it for about 45–60 minutes, or until the chicken is done and the vegetables are tender.

Serve this piping hot with crusty French bread and a cool tossed salad.

SIMMERED CARROTS AND CHICKEN BREASTS

Nutritionists counsel us that white chicken meat is one of the best kinds of protein we can eat. It is low in cholesterol, low in fat, and low in calories — all of which goes double for carrots, which have no cholesterol, no fat, and even fewer calories.

4 chicken breast halves
Dry bread crumbs
2 tablespoons vegetable oil
½-1 cup stock
2 cups carrot coins

½ teaspoon ground ginger
½ cup milk
Salt and pepper to taste
2 tablespoons chopped parsley

Remove the skin and fat from the chicken, roll the pieces in the bread crumbs, and set them aside. Heat the oil in a heavy, covered pan, and brown the chicken pieces on both sides. Remove the chicken pieces and set them aside.

Lower the heat and add ½ cup of stock and stir to blend it well with the pan juices. (Add the remainder of the stock later if the chicken gets too dry as it cooks.)

Now arrange the chicken pieces and the carrot coins in the pan, cover tightly and simmer until the chicken is done and the carrots are tender.

Remove the chicken to a heated serving dish and keep it warm while you stir the ginger and milk into the ingredients remaining in the pan.

Cook this mixture, stirring constantly, until the sauce has thickened to your liking, adding a little more milk if it gets too heavy.

Check the seasonings, adding salt and pepper to taste, spoon the sauce over the warm chicken pieces, and garnish with chopped parsley as you serve the dish.

CHICKEN COLORATURA

A glance at the ingredients for this main dish is like looking into a box of crayons: Dark brown soy sauce, golden honey, orange carrots, white onion, green pepper, yellow butter or margarine, and red wine. The recipe is easy to put together and it is good reheated.

3 tablespoons soy sauce
2 tablespoons honey
$^2/_3$ cup water
1 cup grated carrot
½ cup diced onion
½ cup diced green pepper

3 tablespoons butter or margarine
4 chicken breast halves
3 teaspoons flour
2 tablespoons red wine
Salt and pepper to taste
Noodles or rice

Mix the soy sauce, honey and water with the carrots, onions and green pepper in a medium sauce pan. Cook until they are crisp/tender. Set them aside.

While they're cooking, remove the skin and fat from the chicken pieces, heat the butter or margarine in the frying pan, and sauté the chicken until it is golden brown. Remove and set it aside while you add the flour to the butter or margarine left in the pan, stirring it until it is bubbly and smooth.

Gradually add the vegetables to the flour mix-ture, stirring constantly to keep lumps from form-ing. Stir in the wine.

Arrange the chicken pieces in the vegetable sauce and simmer over low heat until the chicken is done — about 20–30 minutes — adding a little water if necessary to keep the sauce from getting too thick.

Correct the seasonings and serve at once over noodles or rice cooked according to the directions on the package.

MÉLANGE CRÉCY

Carrot Hash *is far too dull a description of this super simple, super good main-course dish... made from leftovers!*

2 tablespoons butter or margarine
1 medium onion, sliced thinly
2 cups cooked carrots, diced
2 cups cooked potatoes, diced
2 cups cooked meat, diced

⅛ teaspoon rosemary
⅛ teaspoon cumin
Salt and pepper to taste
Water or cream

Melt the butter or margarine in a medium-large frying pan. Sauté the onion until it is translucent and tender.

Add the carrots, potatoes, diced meat and seasonings. Mix well with the onion in the frying pan, cover the pan tightly, and cook over low heat until the mixture is brown and crusty on bottom, but still soft on top.

If the hash threatens to stick or burn, add a few drops of water or cream.

When everything is properly *melangee* (mixed) and too hot to eat, serve at once and eat it anyway.

GRANDPA HENDRICKSON'S MUTTON STEW

PREPARATION: 15 MINUTES   **COOKING: 2–4 HOURS**   **SERVES: 4–6**

Grandma *Hendrickson* did the cooking, ordinarily, but sometimes Grandpa *Hendrickson* would get a yen for what he called "some good old-fashioned Swedish mutton stew." He would shoo Grandma out of the kitchen so he could make it the way he wanted it. He used to start the stew simmering in the morning so it would be ready around noon when the main meal of the day was served. We have to agree that there's hardly anything more inviting than a house filled with the aromas coming from a slowly simmering stew pot.

2 tablespoons vegetable oil
2 pounds lean cubed lamb (mutton)
¼ cup flour
Salt and pepper to taste
¼ teaspoon thyme
¼ teaspoon rosemary
1 bay leaf

4–6 cups water
1 stalk celery, diced
4 medium carrots, coined
4 medium potatoes, cubed
1 medium onion, diced
1 medium turnip, diced

Put the oil in a large, heavy, covered pot to heat. Dredge the lamb cubes in the flour to which the salt, pepper, thyme, and rosemary have been added.

(A neat way to do this usually messy job is to put the flour, seasonings and meat into a paper bag, close the top, and shake well.)

Sear the meat on all sides, reduce the heat, add the bay leaf, and gradually stir in four cups of the water, making sure no lumps form. Then add the celery, carrots, potatoes, onion, and turnip.

Cover the pot tightly and simmer gently for 2–4 hours or longer. Add additional water if it gets too thick.

Remove the bay leaf, correct the seasonings and serve.

SHORT RIBS AND LOOOOOOONG CARROTS

PREPARATION: 15 MINUTES   **ROASTING: 1½-2 HOURS**   **SERVES: 4**

Weight-conscious diners often shy away from short ribs, because they are usually just too fatty to eat. But if they are prepared properly — as they are in this recipe — the fat can be removed while the good lean beef remains. There's no worry about fat with carrots, of course, and they have so few calories that it would be almost impossible to gain any weight from eating them.

8-12 3-inch pieces of short rib, with fat removed
Salt and pepper to taste
½ teaspoon marjoram
1 teaspoon rosemary
1 cup water

8 small carrots, whole
4 small potatoes, whole
2 tablespoons flour
4 tablespoons water
½ cup dry red wine

Preheat oven to 325°F.

In a heavy oven-proof pan sear the short ribs, browning them well on all sides. Add the salt and pepper, marjoram, rosemary, and one cup of water. Cover the pan and place it in the oven to roast until meat is tender, about one hour.

Remove the short ribs and set them aside. Cool the pan juices, chill, and remove all the fat that hardens and rises to the surface. In the meantime, trim as much fat as possible from the cooked short ribs.

Return the trimmed short ribs to the pan and place the whole carrots and potatoes on the top and around the sides. Cover the pan and roast until the vegetables are tender, about 45-60 minutes.

Remove the vegetables and the short ribs and arrange them on a serving platter or in a bowl. Keep them warm in the oven.

In a small mixing bowl, combine the flour and the four tablespoons of water to make a smooth paste. Stir this a little at a time into the pan juices, which have been brought to the boil on the stove top. Stir or whisk constantly as the gravy cooks, to keep lumps from forming, until it reaches the consistency of a light sauce. Stir in the dry red wine.

If you find you have added too much of the thickening paste, thin the sauce with a little water.

Correct the seasonings, pour the sauce over the short ribs and vegetables, and serve at once, or serve the sauce in a gravy boat on the side.

BARBECUED CARROT DINNER

PREPARATION: 20 MINUTES   **COOKING: 1½-2 HOURS**   **SERVES: 4**

This recipe could be described as a TV dinner, a meal-in-one, or the like. Whatever you call it, it's good eating! And the fact that it's cooked in one piece of aluminum foil (meaning no messy clean-up chores), makes it taste even better to the cook or the chef.

18-24-inch-wide aluminum foil
1 pound beef steak in 1-inch cubes
4 medium potatoes, quartered
1 large onion, quartered
4 large carrots, quartered
1 green pepper, quartered

½ pound mushrooms
Salt and pepper to taste
1 can cream of mushroom soup
½ soup can of water
4 tablespoons butter or margarine
1 teaspoon fresh parsley, minced

Preheat outdoor grill to white ash stage.

Cut four 42-inch lengths of foil and fold in half, and arrange equal portions of meat, potatoes, onion, carrots, green peppers and mushrooms in the center. Add salt and pepper to taste.

Combine the soup and water and pour in equal parts over the other ingredients, topping with a dab of butter or margarine and a sprinkle of parsley.

Double-fold the top and ends of the foil to seal it securely, and place in center of charcoal grill. Cover and cook until the meat and vegetables are tender, about 1½-2 hours, depending on your fire.

Serve in the foil to hungry picnickers.

CORNED BEEF AND CARROTS

"Necessity is the mother of invention," it is said, and we have to believe that this dinner was invented by early New England settlers because they had neither the time, the patience, nor the crockery and flatware to serve more than one-course meals.

2-3-pound corned beef brisket
Water to cover
1 bay leaf
½ teaspoon thyme
¼ teaspoon rosemary
2 onions, quartered

2 turnips, quartered
5 carrots, halved
3 potatoes, quartered
1 small cabbage, quartered
Salt and pepper to taste
Parsley fronds

Cover the beef with water in a large pot, and add the bay leaf, thyme and rosemary. Cover the pot and cook the brisket for about four hours, or until the meat is fork tender. Remove and set it aside.

Return the water to the boil, add the onions, turnips, and carrots, and cook until they are crisp-tender. Add the potatoes and cook until they are nearly done. Finally, add the cabbage quarters. When the cabbage is just tender, check the seasonings and add salt and pepper to taste.

Return the meat to the pot and heat it through, then arrange the meat and vegetables on a platter, garnish with the parsley fronds and serve.

SLUMGULLION

PREPARATION: 15-20 MINUTES   **COOKING: 20-30 MINUTES**   **SERVES: 4-6**

This is probably not a "classic" slumgullion, if there is such a thing, but it's the way we had it when we were kids. In our view, the rule with slumgullion is: "Anything goes."

8 ounces macaroni, any shape
1½ cups green beans
1½ cups carrot coins
1 pound lean ground beef
½ cup diced onion
¼ cup minced parsley
Dash garlic powder

½ teaspoon oregano
⅛ teaspoon marjoram
1 teaspoon caraway seeds
Dash of sage
4 cups tomato pieces
Salt and pepper to taste
½ cup grated sharp cheese

Cook the macaroni according to the package directions. Drain and set it aside. Cook the green beans in as little water as possible until they are crisp/tender and set them aside. Do the same with the carrot coins.

Meanwhile, sauté the ground beef and onion in a good-sized covered pot or frying pan until the beef is brown and the onions are soft. Stir in the parsley, garlic powder, oregano, marjoram, caraway seeds and sage.

Add the tomato pieces, macaroni, green beans, carrots and salt and pepper to taste. Simmer for 20-30 minutes. Just before you are ready to serve, stir in the grated cheese.

BUSY DAY DINNER

PREPARATION: 10-15 MINUTES   **COOKING: 4-6 HOURS**   **SERVES: 4-8**

Start this meal some day when you have a million other things to do. It takes just minutes to get the ingredients ready, pop them into the pot at the appointed times, and then enjoy the mouth-watering aromas that will be wafting about while the million other things are being done. It can be cooked in the oven or on the stove top. It will be just as good if things are delayed as if you were able to get everyone to the table at just the time you planned. And leftovers from this dish — if you are lucky enough to have any — will make wonderful hash, or should we say "mélange?" See recipe on p. 78.

2-3 pound beef pot roast
4 medium carrots, quartered
4 medium potatoes, whole
2 stalks celery, quartered
4 small onions

2 tablespoons minced parsley
Salt and pepper to taste
4 cups tomato pieces
1½ cups green lima beans

Heat a heavy covered pan or stew pot until a drop of water sizzles on the surface. Sear the roast on all sides, then lower the heat, cover the pan, and cook at low heat for about 2 hours.

Leaving the heat on low, add the carrots, potatoes, celery, and onions. Stir in the parsley, the other seasonings, and the tomatoes. Cover the pot again, and continue cooking at low heat until everything is tender (1–2 hours).

Finally, add the lima beans and continue cooking until they are tender. Correct the seasonings.

Arrange the vegetables and meat on a warmed platter, pour the pan juices into a gravy pitcher and serve at once.

CHILI CON CARROT

One of the greatest things about carrots is their adaptability. Though their color is flashy and distinctive their flavor is mild and unobtrusive. In the recipe that follows the carrots add sweetness and bulk, moderating the acidity of the tomatoes and allowing you to use much less meat than you would otherwise need for balance.

½ pound lean ground beef
2 large carrots, diced
1 large onion, diced
1 16-ounce can tomato pieces
1 20-ounce can tomato purée

2 cups water
3 16-ounce cans kidney beans, including liquid
1½ tablespoons chili powder, or to taste
Salt and pepper to taste

In a large saucepan, sauté the beef until it is brown. Add the carrots and the onion and cook them until the onion is tender.

If any fat has accumulated, drain it off, and add the tomato pieces, tomato purée, kidney beans, and as much of the water as is necessary to make the consistency you like.

(We like chili that is simmered for a couple of hours, so we add all the water called for above, knowing that some of it will boil off during the cooking process.)

Add the chili powder, salt and pepper to your taste and simmer for at least one hour, stirring occasionally to keep the beans from sticking.

Serve piping hot with large slabs of *Staff of Life Carrot Yeast Bread* or *Cheery Carrot Corn Bread.* Delicious! (Leftovers, reheated, are super - see p. 87.)

CARROTY CRACKERY MEAT LOAF

PREPARATION: 15 MINUTES   **BAKING: 45-60 MINUTES**   **SERVES: 4-6**

This meat loaf is so good, we advise you to double everything so you'll be sure to have enough for second helpings and leftovers!

2-3 large carrots
2 eggs
¾ cup milk
3 slices bread, cubed
½ teaspoon celery seeds
½ teaspoon sage
Dash garlic salt

¼ teaspoon poultry seasoning
Salt and pepper to taste
4 tablespoons minced parsley
1 small onion, minced
1½ pounds lean ground beef
8-10 soda crackers
1 cup hot water

Preheat oven to 375°F.

Cook the carrots in as little boiling water as possible, transfer them to a large mixing bowl along with the water they are cooked in, and mash them as you would potatoes.

Combine the carrots, eggs, milk, bread, seasonings, parsley and onion, and beat until all are well blended. Add the ground beef and mix all the ingredients together so they are blended and evenly distributed.

(Don't be bashful. Mix this with your hands. They're easy to wash.)

Crush the crackers to fine-medium crumbs. Form the meat loaf mixture into a round or oblong loaf and roll it in the cracker crumbs until all are taken up.

Place the loaf in a shallow baking pan and pour around it, but not over it, 1 cup of very hot water. Bake for 45–60 minutes or until well done.

POMMES DE TERRE ANNA

Preparation: 15 Minutes

Since you have the whole oven heated up for the meat loaf, you might as well save energy and cook the rest of your meal in there, too.

We usually have baked potatoes (served with sour cream and chives), scalloped potatoes, or, most scrumptious of all, and a wonderfully continental accompaniment for such an everyday dish as meat loaf — *Pommes de Terre Anna.* They're easier than they sound.

The oven setting is the same as that for the meat loaf — 375 degrees F. The ingredients are simple: 4-6 medium potatoes, ¼ pound butter or margarine, ½ teaspoon prepared mustard, *un soupçon d'ail* (just a touch of minced garlic).

Butter a shallow baking dish large enough to hold the potatoes.

Melt the butter or margarine and mix it with the mustard and garlic, and then set the mixture aside while you peel the potatoes and slice them very thin.

Arrange the potatoes in the baking dish so that the slices overlap, covering the bottom and sides of the pan evenly.

As each layer is completed, brush it with the butter/mustard mixture.

When all the potato slices have been arranged in layers, brush the remaining butter/mustard mixture on the top layer, and pop the baking pan into the oven alongside the meat loaf to bake for 40-50 minutes, or until the potatoes are crusty on the outside and tender on the inside.

Given the time to prepare them, they should be done at about the same time as the meat loaf. They can be unmolded onto a platter for serving, or brought to the table as is, and served from the baking dish.

For a side dish, consider *Winter Squash and Carrots* (p. 111) or *Escalloped Asparagus and Carrots* (p. 107).

MEXICARROT CASSEROLE

PREPARATION: 5-10 MINUTES   **BAKING: 30-45 MINUTES**   **SERVES: 4-6**

½ recipe leftover *Chili con Carrot* (see p. 85)
1 cup grated cheese

4 cups corn chips
3 tablespoons chili sauce

Preheat oven to 350°F.

In a large oven-proof casserole, make alternating layers of *Chili con Carrot,* grated cheese, and corn chips, until all ingredients are used up.

(It should work out to at least two layers of each item, ending with the corn chips.)

Just before you put it into the oven, sprinkle the chili sauce over the top.

Bake for 30-45 minutes, or until the mixture is bubbling hot and the cheese is melted.

CATTLE DRIVE CASSEROLE

PREPARATION: 25 MINUTES   **BAKING: 45-60 MINUTES**   **SERVES: 4-6**

We have spent days in the saddle trailing a herd of cantankerous cows through rugged cattle drive country, so we know how heavenly this down-to-earth casserole can taste. Cowhands young and old, experienced and green, tough and tender, will almost fight to get served first when the camp cook calls out: "Come and get it!"

The ingredients for most dishes on the drive come from cans, because there's no electricity for refrigeration out on the trail. Meat, eggs and fresh produce are kept cool for the first few days in portable ice chests.

If you want the casserole to taste as much as possible like the camp cook's version, prepare it in a cast-iron dutch oven. Serve it with a platter of steaming mashed potatoes, hot sourdough biscuits slathered in butter, and a bowl of crisp coleslaw on the side. For dessert: the camp cook's friend and favorite, cool canned peaches.

1½ pounds lean ground beef
1 medium potato, grated
1 small onion, minced
1 celery stalk, diced
1 large carrot, grated
1 slice bread, crumbled
2 eggs, beaten

Salt and pepper to taste
2 tablespoons vegetable oil
1 can cream of mushroom soup
½ can of water
½ cup evaporated milk
2 4-ounce cans mushrooms
½ cup diced green onion

Preheat oven to 350°F.

Combine the beef, potato, onion, celery, carrot, bread, eggs, and salt and pepper, mixing together as you would for a meat loaf.

Heat the oil in a large frying pan. When it is ready, form the meat mixture into 16 balls (about the size of golf balls) and brown them all over.

While they're browning, get out a mixing bowl and beat together the soup, the water and the milk until the mixture is smooth, and then add the mushrooms and the mushroom liquid.

When the meatballs are browned and the sauce is ready, scoop out the meatballs carefully so you don't get any fat that has accumulated, arrange the meatballs in a good-sized covered casserole pan, and pour the mushroom sauce over the meatballs. Cover the pan and pop it into the oven for 45–60 minutes. Check it once in a while to make sure the meatballs aren't sticking, and add a little water if you think the sauce is getting too thick.

When all is ready, sprinkle the green onions over the top of the meatballs and sauce, call the cowhands and stand back to avoid the stampede.

CARROT-BEEF SUKIYAKI

PREPARATION: 20-25 MINUTES   **COOKING: 20-25 MINUTES**   **SERVES: 4-6**

Serve this with rice and other Oriental accompaniments for an outstandingly good (and good for you) meal. Carrots, spinach and celery all have beta-carotene, with the carrots, of course, at the top of the list.

¾ pound round steak
10 ounces fresh or 1 package frozen spinach
1 cup carrots, cut on slant
1 cup celery, cut on slant
½ cup green onions, diced
1 tablespoon vegetable oil

2 tablespoons flour
1-2 cups beef broth
½ pound mushrooms
1-2 tablespoons soy sauce
Salt and pepper to taste

Trim the fat from the steak and discard it. Put the meat into the freezer to firm up for easier slicing.

Partially thaw the spinach, chop it fine, and squeeze it in paper towels to remove excess liquid. Set this aside.

Sauté the carrots, celery and onions in the vegetable oil, cooking just to the crisp/tender stage. Remove from the pan and set them aside.

Slice the meat into thin strips and brown them in the remaining oil in small amounts so there is plenty of room in the pan for them to be seared

and browned. Set them aside as they are browned.

When all the pieces are browned, return them to the pan, sprinkle flour over the meat, and stir over medium to high heat until the flour is brown.

Lower the heat and add the mushrooms and 1 cup of the broth. Stir constantly until a smooth, medium gravy is formed. If necessary to get the proper consistency, add more broth.

Stir in the reserved spinach and the other vegetables, along with the soy sauce and salt and pepper to taste. Cook until the spinach is tender. Serve at once.

BOEUF EN DAUBE

PREPARATION: 30 MINUTES   MARINATE: OVERNIGHT   COOKING: 4-6 HOURS   SERVES: 6-8

One of our favorite books, To the Lighthouse, *by Virginia Woolf, has a passage describing an entrée —
a beef stew — which takes two days to prepare. We often make the dish for special occasions and special
people. The time taken to get it ready is worth it. The longer you can let these ingredients marinate and
simmer together, the better the results.*

2 pounds sirloin tip steak
¾ cup dry red wine
1 medium carrot, coined
1 small onion, diced
1 bay leaf
3 peppercorns
2 tablespoons Worcestershire sauce
¼ cup minced parsley
¼ teaspoon minced garlic
3 tablespoons vegetable oil

3 tablespoons flour
1¼ cups dry red wine
2-4 cups beef broth
Salt and pepper to taste
½ teaspoon thyme
Dash of cumin
4 medium carrots in 1-inch chunks
10-12 small onions, whole
½ pound mushrooms, whole
6 small potatoes, quartered

Preheat oven to 350°F (optional).

The day before you plan to serve your *Boeuf en Daube,* trim all the fat from the steak, cut it into two-inch pieces, and place it in a covered glass or porcelain bowl. Set it aside.

In another bowl, combine the wine, carrot coins, diced onion, bay leaf, peppercorns, Worcestershire sauce, parsley, and garlic. Pour this mixture over the steak cubes and press the meat down into the marinade. Cover the dish and place it in the refrigerator for overnight. Baste the meat occasionally to ensure that all the chunks are reached

equally by the wine mixture.

The day of your dinner, remove the meat and drain it thoroughly. Drain the vegetables and discard the bay leaf and peppercorns, reserving the vegetables and the liquid. Set them aside.

Dry the meat chunks by pressing them between layers of paper toweling.

Heat the oil in a heavy covered pot or large frying pan until it sizzles when you flick a drop of water into it. Add the drained and dried meat chunks and sear them on all sides.

Sprinkle the flour over the meat and stir until

the flour is browned but not burned. Lower the heat, add the reserved marinade, the marinated vegetables, the additional wine, and enough broth to make s light gravy, about two cups.

Stir in the salt and pepper to taste, the thyme and cumin, and let this mixture simmer at the lowest heat possible for at least four hours, either on top of the stove or in the oven. Stir it occasionally.

About two hours before you plan to eat, prepare the carrots, onions, mushrooms, and potatoes, and add them to the pot.

Stir the *daube* occasionally to make sure it is not sticking. Add more broth as necessary to keep the sauce at the right consistency — light but not thin. Check the seasonings and correct them to your taste.

At the last minute toss a green salad, set out a basket of French bread and hard rolls, and your meal is complete.

JACK'S CARROT-BEEF-BURGERS

PREPARATION: 12-15 MINUTES   **COOKING: 10-15 MINUTES**   **SERVES: 4-6**

The most expensive ingredient in this recipe — the ground beef — is stretched by combining it with carrots, wheat germ and tofu. We serve it with bright green peas, steamed brown rice, and Gold Sovereign Salad *(p. 59).*

1 egg
2 tablespoons milk
¼ cup wheat germ
½ cup grated carrots
¼ teaspoon sage

Salt and pepper to taste
¼ cup minced onion
1 pound lean ground beef
½ cup medium tofu

Beat together the egg, milk, and wheat germ, add the carrots, seasonings, and onion, and mix well. Add the ground beef and tofu and work all the ingredients together thoroughly.

Shape the mixture into four to six patties and fry on a griddle or in a frying pan over medium heat until they are brown on the outside and as done as you like on the inside.

CARROT STROGANOFF

PREPARATION: 15 MINUTES   **COOKING: 30-45 MINUTES**   **SERVES: 4-6**

Carrots are right at home in a Stroganoff-type entrée, since according to some experts, they origi- nated in Eastern Russia. From there they were introduced into Europe, North and South America and the Orient, finally coming to the New World in the middle of the 17th Century. This particular Stroganoff is a hearty mixture that is absolutely sensational served with wide buttered noodles or smooth mashed pota- toes. Nasdrovia!

2 tablespoons butter or margarine
¾ pound lean round steak, cut in 1-inch cubes
¼ cup diced onion
2 tablespoons flour
1–2 cups beef broth
2 cups carrot coins

½ pound whole mushrooms
¼ teaspoon sweet basil
Salt and pepper to taste
½ cup dry white wine
1 cup commercial sour cream

Heat the butter or margarine in a covered pot and sear the beef on all sides. Add the onions to the pan and cook them until they are soft. Remove the beef and onions and set them aside.

Sprinkle the flour into the butter or margarine remaining in the pan and stir until it is bubbling. Gradually stir in enough of the broth to make a light gravy.

Return the beef and onions to the pan with the gravy, add the carrots and mushrooms, sweet basil, and salt and pepper to taste. Simmer until the beef is fork-tender — about 30–45 minutes.

Just before serving, add the wine, and fold in the sour cream. Reheat the mixture, but do not let it come to the boil. When it is heated through, serve at once.

SIDE
DISHES
CHAPTER 9

CALICO RICE

Plain brown rice is dolled-up and delicious when it combines with deep orange carrots, beige mushrooms, pale green celery, white onion, and bright green parsley. It can be served as a main course for a meatless meal, or as a side dish.

2 tablespoons vegetable oil
½ cup onion, diced
½ cup celery, diced
2 tablespoons flour
3 cups water
1 cup brown rice

1 cup grated carrots
½ pound mushrooms
¼ teaspoon sage
2 tablespoons parsley, minced
Salt and pepper to taste

Heat the oil in a large pot or frying pan and cook the onions and celery until they are just translucent. Remove and set them aside.

Add the flour to the oil remaining in the pan, stir it until it is bubbling and beginning to brown, then slowly add the water. Stir this mixture to make a smooth sauce.

Add the rice and all the other ingredients to the sauce, mixing them well. Cover the pan and simmer until the rice is done and the water is absorbed. Add more water if necessary.

Correct the seasonings and serve at once.

CARROT COINS AND GREEN PEAS

PREPARATION: 15-20 MINUTES   **SERVES: 4-6**

Peas and carrots are often combined in one side dish, and one reason for the combination is the way their colors complement each other. Here, we've enhanced both their looks and their flavors with the addition of green onion, celery leaves and brown sugar.

3 cups carrot coins
¼ cup fresh celery leaves
1 tablespoon green onion, diced
Salt to taste

1 tablespoon butter or margarine
1 tablespoon brown sugar
¾ cup water
1 cup fresh or frozen peas

In a medium saucepan place the carrots, celery leaves, green onion, salt, butter or margarine, brown sugar, and water.

Cover the pan tightly and simmer until the car-rots are crisp/tender. Add the peas and continue cooking for 2-3 minutes, or until the peas are tender.

Serve at once.

CARROT AND APPLE BAKE

PREPARATION: 5-10 MINUTES   **BAKING: 20-30 MINUTES**   **SERVES: 4**

How a dish looks is almost as important as how it tastes and smells. Here, bright orange carrots, red and white apples, and tart yellow lemon combine colors, textures, aromas and tastes.

2 cups thin carrot coins
2 medium apples, diced
⅛ cup minced onion
Salt to taste

2 tablespoons brown sugar
¼ cup water
2 tablespoons butter or margarine
4 thin lemon slices

Preheat oven to 375°F.

In a covered casserole combine the carrots, apples, onion, salt and brown sugar. Mix them together well.

Add the water, dot the mixture with butter or margarine and top with the lemon slices. Cover the casserole and bake for 20 to 30 minutes, or until the carrots are tender.

Serve at once.

CARROT LATKES

PREPARATION: 10-15 MINUTES   **COOKING: 5-10 MINUTES**   **SERVES: 4**

A friend who is a sabra — *a native-born Israeli — introduced us to the basic recipe for this dish. She makes it with 2 cups of mashed potatoes. We use half carrots and half potatoes to make it more colorful and more nutritious.*

1 cup cooked mashed carrots
1 cup cooked mashed potatoes
1 small onion, minced

¼ cup plain yogurt
3 eggs, beaten
Salt and pepper to taste

In a medium mixing bowl combine the carrots, potatoes, onions and yogurt.

Add the eggs, salt and pepper, and mix until all the ingredients are blended.

Drop the mixture by tablespoonsful onto a hot oiled griddle and cook until they are brown and crispy on both sides.

Serve the latkes hot, as you would potato pancakes, with meat dishes or other entrées.

CARROT PATTIES

PREPARATION: 15-20 MINUTES   **SERVES: 4**

These patties can substitute for your meat dish since they have egg protein in them, or they can be served alongside a meat, cheese or vegetable-based entrée.

¼ cup flour
2 tablespoons chopped parsley
¼ cup minced green onion
Salt and pepper to taste

¼ teaspoon grated lemon peel
Dash of tabasco
2 eggs, slightly beaten
3 cups grated carrots

In a medium bowl combine the flour, parsley, onion, salt and pepper, lemon peel and tabasco.
Stir in the eggs and carrots and mix them well.
Drop the mixture by heaping tablespoonsful onto a lightly greased griddle or skillet.

Cook the patties over medium heat for about 5 minutes, or until they are brown on one side. Turn them over and brown the other side.
Serve at once.

CARROTS ORANGE, PARSLEY GREEN

PREPARATION: 15-20 MINUTES   **SERVES: 4-6**

Carrots and parsley are a pair of the plant world's "kissing cousins," so to speak, so it's no wonder they get along so well together in this simple and simply delicious side dish.

4 tablespoons butter or margarine
4 cups carrot coins
2 tablespoons honey

Salt and pepper to taste
½ cup water
3 tablespoons parsley, chopped

Heat the butter or margarine in a medium saucepan. Add the carrots and honey and sprinkle them with salt and pepper.

Add the water, cover the pan, and simmer the carrots for 10–15 minutes, or until they are nearly tender.

Uncover the saucepan and cook the carrots over medium heat. Stir them occasionally. When the water has evaporated and the carrots are tender stir in the parsley and serve at once.

CARROT CASSEROLE

PREPARATION: 10-15 MINUTES   **BAKING: 15-25 MINUTES**   **SERVES: 4**

This bubbling dish has just a touch of nippy horseradish to warm the cockles of the heart and bring out some of the possibilities of the carrot that perhaps you hadn't realized were there.

2 cups carrot coins
2 tablespoons butter or margarine
1½ tablespoons minced onion
½ teaspoon dry horseradish
2 tablespoons minced parsley

Salt and pepper to taste
¼ cup carrot cooking liquid
1 cup grated cheese
⅓ cup fine bread crumbs

Preheat oven to 375°F.

Cook the carrots until they are crisp/tender. Drain them and reserve the liquid. While the carrots are cooking, melt the butter in a medium saucepan and sauté the onion until it is soft.

Combine the carrots and onions in an oiled, covered casserole, and sprinkle them with the horseradish, parsley, salt and pepper and ¼ cup of the reserved cooking liquid.

Sprinkle on the grated cheese and cover the top with bread crumbs. Bake the casserole for about 15 minutes, covered. Add a little more carrot liquid if you think it is getting too dry.

Remove the cover and continue baking for 5–10 minutes, or until it is golden brown on top. Serve at once.

CARROT TIMBALES

PREPARATION: 15 MINUTES   **BAKING: 30-40 MINUTES**   **SERVES: 4-6**

The word timbale *comes from the French for* kettledrum. *Originally this creamy mixture of chicken, lobster, cheese or fish was cooked in a drum-shaped mold or in a small pastry shell. If you don't happen to have an oven-proof kettledrum on hand, use custard cups or a ring mold instead.*

2 eggs
¼ cup milk
Salt and pepper to taste
2½ cups cooked puréed carrots
1 tablespoon minced parsley

½ cup soft bread crumbs
¼ cup minced onion
1 tablespoon melted butter or margarine
Parsley sprigs

Preheat oven to 350°F.

Beat the eggs in a large bowl with the milk until they are frothy and light. Add the salt and pepper, carrots, minced parsley, bread crumbs and onion. Beat together until they are well blended.

Pour the mixture into custard cups or a ring mold which have been brushed with the melted butter or margarine. Fill the cups or the mold two-thirds full. Place the cups or ring mold in a shallow baking pan with enough boiling water to come halfway up the sides of the cups or the mold.

Bake the timbales for 30–40 minutes, or until they are firm. Serve in the cups or unmold the ring onto a platter.

Garnish the dish with a sprig of parsley and serve at once.

CARROT SOUFFLÉ

Egg-based dishes are not as popular as they used to be, now that we all know the dangers of too much cholesterol. But this soufflé calls for only three eggs and it will serve as many as six people. In addition, each serving has a healthy dose of the carrots that are nature's best source of beta-carotene.

2 tablespoons butter or margarine
3 tablespoons flour
½ cup milk
4 cups grated carrots

3 egg yolks
2 tablespoons minced parsley
Salt and pepper to taste
3 egg whites

Preheat oven to 350°F.

Melt the butter in a medium saucepan, stir in the flour to make a smooth paste, and then blend in the milk and cook until thickened. Set the pan aside to cool.

In a medium mixing bowl combine the carrots, egg yolks, parsley, salt, and pepper. Combine with the cooled flour mixture. Set aside.

Beat the egg whites until stiff, and fold them into the carrot mixture.

Pour the mixture into a buttered 1½–2-quart soufflé dish. Set the dish in a shallow pan of hot water and bake for 25–35 minutes, or until a kitchen knife inserted in the center comes out clean.

CREAMED CARROTS

This basic recipe for a plain and simple carrot side dish has probably been one of your old standbys. We give it a new lease on life with a hint of honey and a dash of nutmeg.

4 carrots, diced
2 tablespoons honey
1½ cups water
2 tablespoons butter or margarine

2 tablespoons flour
⅓ cup dry milk solids
Dash nutmeg
Salt and pepper to taste

Place the carrots, honey and water in a covered saucepan and cook them until the carrots are tender. Drain them, reserving the liquid, and set it aside.

In another saucepan melt the butter or margarine, add the flour and stir to a smooth paste. Blend in one cup of the liquid from the carrots, the dry milk solids, and the nutmeg.

Cook the mixture over low heat, stirring it constantly to keep it from forming lumps. If it becomes too thick, add more of the carrot liquid.

When the sauce is thickened, add the carrots, salt and pepper to taste, and serve at once.

GLAZED CARROTS

PREPARATION: 15-20 MINUTES   **SERVES: 4**

Carrots are naturally sweet — five to ten percent of their weight consists of sugar. You may want to reduce the amounts of sugar and molasses in this recipe, once you've tried and tested it yourself.

4 medium carrots
2 tablespoons butter or margarine
1 tablespoon molasses

2 tablespoons sugar
Salt to taste

Cut the carrots into shoestrings about 2 inches long and add to the butter in a covered saucepan. Stir in the molasses and sugar.

Add the salt to taste, cover, and simmer until the carrots are tender but not mushy.
Toss to cover with the glaze and serve at once.

FRESH CARROT PUFF

PREPARATION: 10-15 MINUTES   **BAKING: 30-35 MINUTES**   **SERVES: 4**

1 pound carrots, peeled and quartered
2 tablespoons milk
2 eggs, beaten
Salt and pepper to taste
¼ teaspoon sugar

Dash cloves
2 tablespoons butter or margarine
⅓ cup onion, minced
2 tablespoons fresh parsley, chopped

Preheat oven to 350°F.
In a covered medium saucepan, cook the carrots in boiling water until they are tender. Drain, place the carrots in a small mixing bowl, and beat them with an electric mixer until they are smooth.
Beat in the milk, egg, salt and pepper, sugar,

and cloves.
Melt the butter in a small saucepan, add the onion and parsley, and cook until the onion is tender. Stir into the carrot mixture.
Turn the mixture into a buttered 1-quart casserole and bake for 30–35 minutes, or until set.

CARROTS SEETHED IN RED WINE

PREPARATION: 15-20 MINUTES   **SERVES: 4**

The adaptable carrot can get along with just about any other ingredients you want to put with it. Here, it settles in happily with wine, spices, honey, nuts and butter.

3 cups carrot coins
½ cup water
¼ cup red wine
Dash cinnamon
Dash cloves

Salt to taste
2 tablespoons honey
¼ cup chopped nuts
2 tablespoons butter

Combine the carrots, water, wine, cinnamon, cloves, salt to taste, and honey in a saucepan and simmer until the carrots are tender and the liquid is nearly gone.

Increase the heat to evaporate the remaining liquid, but be careful not to let the carrots stick or burn.

Remove the pan from the heat, stir in the nuts and butter, and serve immediately.

MASHED CARROTS

PREPARATION: 15-20 MINUTES   **SERVES: 4-6**

Carrots served this way are a pleasant surprise. They're as easy to prepare as common, ordinary mashed potatoes. (Needless to say, such adjectives as "common" and "ordinary" can never be applied to Mashed Carrots. Try "creamy." Try "smooth." Try "delicious." Now you're talking!)

6 medium to large carrots
¼-½ cup milk

Salt and pepper to taste
2-3 tablespoons butter or margarine

Wash and peel the carrots and cook them in as little boiling, salted water as possible until they are tender. Drain, reserving the liquid for later use in soups, gravies and the like.

Now, pretend the carrots are potatoes and mash them in exactly the same way, adding as little milk as necessary to make them light and fluffy.

Season to taste with salt and pepper, turn out into a serving dish and top with butter or margarine.

MOTHER'S CARROT LOAF

PREPARATION: 10–15 MINUTES　　　**BAKING: 60 MINUTES**　　　**SERVES: 4–6**

Like most experienced cooks, Mother wrote her recipes in culinary shorthand. For instance, if a recipe like this one called for eggs, Mother understood that they were not to be thrown into the mixing bowl whole, but must first be cracked, broken shells discarded, whites and yolks beaten together, and then added to the rest of the ingredients.

Herewith, then, is Mother's recipe for Carrot Loaf, *just as she wrote it down so many years ago. Necessary translations are in parentheses.*

2 c. ground (grated) carrots
2 c. (soft) bread cubes
⅔ c. chopped nuts
1 teaspoon salt (or to taste)

2 c. tomatoes, (diced)
2 small onions, (minced)
3 eggs, (beaten)
pepper (to taste)

Preheat oven to 350°F.

Mix (all the ingredients) together (thoroughly in a large mixing bowl) and bake (uncovered) in buttered pan (casserole) for (about) 1 hour (or until the center is firm). Serve (the casserole) with cream sauce (a medium white sauce).

ORIENTAL CARROTS

Oriental cuisine — in nearly every part of the Far East — rivals that of France for subtlety and variety. Both, of course, feature carrots in some of their finest dishes. This one goes well with rice or oriental noodles.

2 tablespoons vegetable oil
2 cups thin carrot coins
1 small can sliced water chestnuts
Beef or chicken broth
1 tablespoon soy sauce or to taste
2 tablespoons wine vinegar
2 tablespoons brown sugar

Salt and pepper to taste
1 tablespoon cornstarch
20 snow peas, fresh or frozen
¼ pound mushrooms, whole
1 cup fresh bean sprouts
¼ cup minced green onion tops or chives

Heat the oil in a medium saucepan. Add the carrots and sauté them until they are just crisp/tender, in the manner of stir-fried vegetables. Remove the carrots from the pan and set them aside.

Drain the water chestnuts, reserving the liquid. Set both of them aside.

In the saucepan, combine the reserved liquid and enough of the broth to make one cup, with the soy sauce, vinegar, brown sugar, salt and pepper. Bring this mixture to a boil.

Meanwhile, mix ¼ cup of the remaining liquid/broth combination with the cornstarch and stir it into the soy sauce mixture a little at a time. Cooking it over a low heat until you have a fine light clear sauce.

To this sauce add the reserved carrots, the reserved water chestnuts, the snow peas, mushrooms and bean sprouts. Continue cooking the mixture for a few minutes longer to ensure that all the ingredients are tender but not overdone.

As you serve the dish, sprinkle over it the minced green onion tops or chives.

ESCALLOPED ASPARAGUS AND CARROTS

Another recipe that Mother must have run across in a newspaper or magazine and copied out in the lined school notebook where she recorded things that interested her. It is an unusual and delicious dish, combining carrots with asparagus, a vegetable that usually likes to go its own way. Ingredients and directions are just as Mother copied them into her notebook. (Our translations are in parentheses.)

1½ tablespoons of fat (butter or margarine)
2 tablespoons flour
1 c. milk
¼ c. of grated cheese

1 c. of asparagus (cooked)
1 c. of carrots (cooked coins)
¼ teaspoon of salt (or to taste)
¾ c. of buttered (fine, dry) bread crumbs

Preheat oven to 375°F.
Scald the milk in a double boiler. Cream the butter and flour and add to the hot milk. Cook in the double boiler for 20 minutes or until it is of a creamy consistency. (Make a white sauce using the butter or margarine, the flour and the milk, stirring until smooth and creamy.)

Remove hot sauce from stove and add grated cheese. Stir until cheese is melted. Add the vegetables (and salt to taste), pour into a baking dish, sprinkle the buttered crumbs over the top and brown in a hot oven (for 15–20 minutes). (Serve at once.)

RING-A-ROUND-A-CARROT

Take rosy orange carrots, wide noodles, and deep green broccoli. Put the carrots and noodles together with a cheesy sauce, wrap them around the broccoli pieces, serve them up to family and friends, and prepare to receive compliments.

4 tablespoons butter or margarine
5 tablespoons flour
1½ cups milk
4 cups cooked wide noodles
¼ cup minced onion
2 cups grated carrots

1 cup sliced mushrooms
Salt and pepper to taste
⅛ teaspoon crushed garlic
1 egg, beaten
1 cup grated sharp cheese
1-2 cups broccoli pieces

Preheat oven to 350°F.

Melt the butter or margarine in a medium saucepan, stir in the flour, and cook until it is bubbling. Add the milk gradually. Stir the mixture until it is thick and creamy. Remove it from the heat and set it aside.

Meanwhile, combine the noodles, onion, carrots and mushrooms in a large mixing bowl. Add the cooled sauce, salt and pepper, garlic, egg, and cheese and mix them well. Pack the mixture into a buttered 9-inch oven-proof ring mold. Bake it for 30–45 minutes, remove the mold from the oven, and let it rest for 10 minutes while you cook the broccoli pieces.

Unmold the carrot-noodle mixture onto a serving plate, drain the broccoli, and mound it in the center of the ring. Add a dab of butter or margarine on top, and serve hot.

SCALLOPED CARROTS

PREPARATION: 15 MINUTES   **BAKING: 20-30 MINUTES**   **SERVES: 4-6**

It's fun and interesting to cook with carrots because they're so colorful. Just a few carrot coins sprinkled through any dish improves its looks. Here, the whole casserole is bright with them.

4 medium carrots, coined
2 tablespoons butter or margarine
2 tablespoons flour
Salt and pepper to taste

1 cup milk
Carrot liquid
¾ cup crushed soda crackers

Preheat oven to 375°F.

Cook the carrots in a medium saucepan until they are tender in just enough salted water to keep them from burning. Drain, reserving liquid, and set aside.

In another saucepan melt the margarine, stir in the flour, salt and pepper, and cook until bubbly.

Gradually add the milk and as much of the carrot liquid (or additional milk) as is necessary to make a smooth, medium sauce.

Place the carrots in a buttered baking dish, pour the sauce over them and top with crushed crackers.

Bake for 20–30 minutes and serve at once.

SWEET AND SIMPLE CASSEROLE

PREPARATION: 10-20 MINUTES   **BAKING: 20-25 MINUTES**   **SERVES: 4**

Now here's a diner's delight: A side dish that is so good for you it could qualify as medicine, yet so delicious it could be classed as a dessert. Both carrots and sweet potatoes are fairly bursting with beta-carotene.

3 medium carrots, coined
1 medium sweet potato, sliced thinly
½ cup orange juice
Salt to taste
3 tablespoons brown sugar

4 tablespoons butter or margarine
¼ teaspoon cinnamon
3 tablespoons grated orange peel
3 tablespoons chopped English walnuts
Orange slices

Preheat oven to 375°F.

In a medium covered saucepan cook the carrots, sweet poatoes, orange juice and salt until the vegetables are just tender.

Add the brown sugar, butter, cinnamon, orange peel and nuts to the carrots and sweet potatoes and toss gently to coat the vegetables.

Turn the mixture into a 1½-quart covered casserole, arrange the orange slices on top and bake, covered, for 20–25 minutes. Serve at once.

ORANGE ROASTED CARROTS

PREPARATION: 5-10 MINUTES   **ROASTING: 15-20 MINUTES**   **SERVES: 4**

Make this easy side dish the next time you use the oven to prepare the entrée for a meal. Cooking two or more dishes with the same oven heat makes using it sensible, especially on chilly days when the house has to be heated anyway.

4 cups shoestring carrots
4 teaspoons butter or margarine
¼ cup orange juice

¼ cup brown sugar
Salt to taste
2 tablespoons minced parsley

Preheat oven to 375°F.

Place the carrots in an oven-proof dish with a cover. Dot them with the butter or margarine.

Mix the orange juice with the brown sugar and salt and pour this mixture over the carrots.

Cover the baking dish and bake for 15–20 minutes, or until the carrots are tender. Add a little more orange juice if the carrots get too dry.

Remove the dish from the oven, sprinkle the carrots with the parsley and serve at once.

WINTER SQUASH AND CARROTS

PREPARATION: 10 MINUTES   **COOKING: 10-15 MINUTES**   **SERVES: 4-6**

Both bright yellow winter squash and deep orange carrots are high in beta-carotene, which gives them their characteristic coloring. When this dish is cooked, it's sometimes hard to tell where the squash leaves off and the carrots begin.

¼-½ cup water
1½ cups thin carrot slices
1½ cups thin slices of any type of winter squash
1 teaspoon honey

4 thin slices lemon
¼ teaspoon cinnamon
1 tablespoon butter or margarine
Salt and pepper to taste

Bring the water to a boil in a medium covered saucepan. Add the carrots, squash, honey, lemon slices and cinnamon.

Return the pot to the boil, reduce the heat and cover the pot. Simmer the carrots and squash un-til they are tender.

Remove the pan from the heat, add the butter or margarine, and toss the vegetables to coat them.

Season to taste with salt and pepper, and serve at once.

BREADS
& MUFFINS
CHAPTER 10

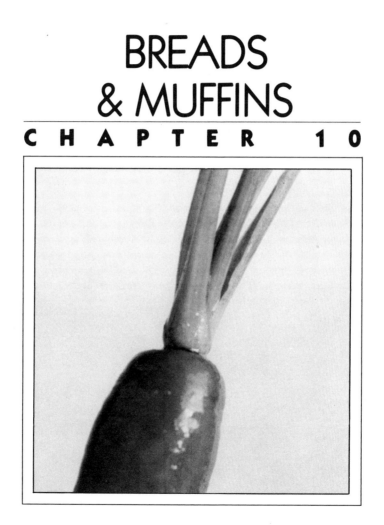

STAFF OF LIFE CARROT YEAST BREAD

PREPARATION: 30-40 MINUTES   RISING: 2-2½ HOURS   BAKING: 30-40 MINUTES
YIELD: TWO 9" LOAVES

When you add carrots to your home-baked bread, you'll find out how much more fun it is to turn out light-orange-colored loaves than ordinary plain white or brown ones. It's like the difference between watching a movie in black and white and then seeing the same film in living color. Incidentally, this bread makes the crustiest toast we know.

1 package dry yeast
1 tablespoon sugar
⅓ cup warm water
2½-3 cups whole wheat flour
2½-3 cups white flour

1 ounce dried carrot flakes
1½ teaspoons salt, or to taste
5 tablespoons melted butter or margarine
1⅔ cups water

Preheat oven to 375°F.

Stir the yeast and sugar into the warm water and let the mixture stand for up to ten minutes, or until a light foam appears.

In a large mixing bowl combine 2½ cups of the whole wheat flour, 2½ cups of the white flour, the carrot flakes, salt, and 4 tablespoons of the butter or margarine. Blend these ingredients thoroughly.

When the yeast has foamed up, combine it with the remaining water and stir it into the dry ingredients until all the moisture is taken up by the flour. Add the additional half cup of each kind of flour, if necessary, to make a stiff dough.

Knead and work the dough until it is smooth and elastic, and then form it into a ball and brush it with the remaining butter or margarine. Leave it in the mixing bowl to rise. Cover the bowl with a sheet of plastic wrap or a damp cloth.

When the dough has risen to double in size, punch it down, form it into two loaves, and place them in two oiled loaf pans. Cover them with plastic wrap or a damp cloth and let the loaves rise to double in bulk.

Bake the loaves on the middle rack in the oven for 30–40 minutes, or until they are golden brown on top and sound hollow when you tap them sharply with your finger tips.

Remove the loaves from the pans and cool them on a rack.

WHOLESOME CARROT BREAD

PREPARATION: 15-20 MINUTES   **BAKING: 45-60 MINUTES**   **YIELD: TWO 8½" LOAVES**

2½ cups whole wheat flour
2 teaspoons salt, or to taste
1 teaspoon baking soda
2 teaspoons baking powder
1 cup granulated sugar
1 cup brown sugar, packed
½ cup wheat germ

1 cup vegetable oil
1 teaspoon vanilla
3 eggs
2 cups grated carrots
½ cup chopped pecans
1 cup raisins

Preheat oven to 350°F.

In a medium bowl combine the flour, salt, baking soda, and baking powder. Set aside. In a large bowl beat the granulated sugar, brown sugar, wheat germ, oil, vanilla, and eggs until they are thick and creamy, and then stir in the dry ingredients until they are moistened. Fold in the carrots, pecans and raisins.

Pour the batter into two oiled and waxed paper-lined loaf pans and bake for 45–60 minutes, or until a tester inserted in the center comes out clean.

Cool the loaves in the pans for 10 minutes. Remove from the pans and cool completely on racks.

JACK ROBINSON CARROT BREAD

PREPARATION: 10 MINUTES   **BAKING: 45-50 MINUTES**   **YIELD: ONE 7½" LOAF**

You can have this bread mixed, baked and onto the rack cooling in what seems to be no time at all.

1 cup puréed carrots
⅓ cup brown sugar
⅓ cup granulated sugar
⅓ cup butter or margarine, softened
2 eggs

2 tablespoons grated orange peel
1¾ cups flour
2¼ teaspoons baking powder
½ teaspoon salt, or to taste
½ cup chopped nuts

Preheat oven to 350°F.

Combine the carrots, sugars, margarine, eggs and orange peel in a large bowl. Set aside.

Mix the flour, baking powder, and salt and blend these into the carrot mixture. Stir in the chopped nuts.

Turn into an oiled loaf pan and bake for 45–50 minutes or until a cake tester inserted in the center of the bread comes out clean. Remove from the pan and cool on a wire rack.

Wrap in foil or plastic wrap and let the loaf stand overnight at room temperature before slicing. Serve with butter or cream cheese.

TWICE-ORANGE LOAF

PREPARATION: 12 MINUTES　　　**BAKING: 50 MINUTES**　　　**YIELD: ONE 9" LOAF**

This delicious, moist, nutritious loaf can be served warm or cold, cut into slices and spread with butter, margarine or cream cheese. (We suggest you double the recipe, so you have one loaf extra to freeze for use when you don't have time to prepare one from scratch.)

1½ cups flour
1 teaspoon baking powder
1 teaspoon cinnamon
¾ cup sugar
1 teaspoon soda
¼ teaspoon salt or to taste

2 eggs
⅔ cup vegetable oil
1 teaspoon vanilla
1 cup shredded carrots
½ cup mashed apricots
¼ cup apricot juice

Preheat the oven to 350°F.

Combine the flour, baking powder, cinnamon, sugar, soda and salt in a medium mixing bowl. Set aside.

In a large mixing bowl, combine the eggs and oil with vanilla and beat or whisk until the mixture is light and frothy.

Add the carrots, mashed apricots and apricot juice to the egg mixture and blend. Then stir in the dry ingredients and mix well.

Pour into an oiled loaf pan and bake for 50–55 minutes, or until a cake tester inserted in the center comes out clean.

GOLDEN CARROT NUT BREAD

PREPARATION: 15 MINUTES   **BAKING: 40-50 MINUTES**   **YIELD: ONE 7½" LOAF**

2 cups flour
⅓ cup sugar
2 teaspoons baking powder
1 teaspoon salt, or to taste
1 cup grated coconut

½ cup chopped walnuts
2 cups grated carrots
2 tablespoons vegetable oil
1 egg, well beaten
¾ cup milk

Preheat oven to 350°F.

Combine the flour, sugar, baking powder, and salt. Sift into a large bowl and stir in the coconut and walnuts. Set aside.

In another bowl beat together the carrots, oil, egg, and milk and mix well. Combine the carrot mixture with the dry ingredients and blend.

Pour the mixture into a buttered and floured loaf pan. Place in the oven and bake for 40–50 minutes or until a cake tester inserted in the center comes out clean. Cool on a rack.

MUFFINS CRÉCY

PREPARATION: 10 MINUTES   **BAKING: 20-25 MINUTES**   **YIELD: 12 MUFFINS**

1¾ cups flour
1 teaspoon baking powder
½ teaspoon baking soda
½ teaspoon salt, or to taste
¼ cup brown sugar

½ cup puréed carrots or puréed carrot baby food
3 tablespoons vegetable oil
1 cup buttermilk
1 egg

Preheat oven to 425°F.

In a medium mixing bowl combine the flour, baking powder, baking soda, and salt.

In another large bowl beat the brown sugar, puréed carrots, oil, buttermilk and egg together, and then add flour mixture and stir just until everything is moistened, but not smoothly blended.

Fill the muffin cups two-thirds full and bake for 20–25 minutes, or until a tester inserted in the center comes out clean. Serve warm.

CHEERY CARROTY CORN BREAD

PREPARATION: 10 MINUTES   **BAKING: 20-25 MINUTES**   **YIELD: ONE 8"x8" PAN**

You will love this crispy, crunchy, bright-colored bread, which tastes as good as it looks. Serve it piping hot with real butter to maximize the beta-carotene benefits. You can substitute puréed carrot baby food in this recipe.

1 cup yellow corn meal
1 teaspoon salt, or to taste
1 cup flour
4 teaspoons baking powder
¼ cup soft butter or margarine

¼ cup sugar
2 eggs
½ cup milk
½ cup puréed carrots

Preheat oven to 400°F.

Combine the corn meal, salt, flour and baking powder in a medium bowl, and mix them well. Set the bowl aside.

In another bowl beat the butter or margarine and sugar until they are light, then add the eggs, milk and carrot purée. Beat the mixture thoroughly after each addition.

Stir the dry ingredients into the carrot mixture and blend them into a smooth batter.

Pour the batter into a well-oiled baking pan, and bake it for 20–25 minutes, or until a toothpick or cake tester inserted in the center comes out clean.

Serve at once.

HARVEST LOAF

PREPARATION: 20 MINUTES   **BAKING: 60 MINUTES**   **YIELD: ONE 9″ LOAF**

1½ cups white flour
1½ cups whole wheat flour
1 teaspoon baking soda
½ teaspoon cinnamon
½ teaspoon cloves
½ teaspoon salt, or to taste
1 egg
½ cup sugar

¼ cup butter or margarine, softened
½ teaspoon maple flavoring
1½ cups grated carrots
1 cup buttermilk
¼ cup orange juice
½ cup raisins
½ cup chopped nuts
1 tablespoon grated lemon peel

Preheat oven to 350°F.

In a large bowl stir together the white flour, whole wheat flour, baking soda, cinnamon, cloves and salt. Set aside. In another bowl beat the egg, sugar, margarine and flavoring until well mixed, and then add the carrots, buttermilk, orange juice, raisins, nuts and lemon peel. Combine the dry ingredients with the carrot mixture, blend well, and turn the batter into an oiled loaf pan.

Bake for one hour or until a tester inserted in the center comes out clean. Cool for ten minutes in the pan, remove, and cool completely on a rack.

DESSERTS

CARROT CHIP COOKIES

PREPARATION: 20 MINUTES   BAKING: 10 MINUTES   YIELD: ABOUT 7 DOZEN COOKIES

Nobody in the whole world but you will ever guess that these cheery, chewy, chippy cookies are any-thing but good-tasting treats. But you will know that in every fast-disappearing batch are two full cups of carrots, the undisputed King of Beta-Carotene. Let the kids and the grown-ups and all the in-betweeners have as many as they want.

In the unlikely event that all these cookies aren't eaten up as fast as they're removed from the cookie sheets, they can be frozen for future use. Put them in a thick plastic bag and make sure it's airtight. About 20 minutes before you plan to serve them, take them out of the freezer and let them thaw at room tem-perature.

2 cups grated carrots
1 cup granulated sugar
1 cup brown sugar, packed
1 cup soft butter or margarine
2 teaspoons vanilla
2 eggs

2 cups white flour
1 cup whole wheat flour
1½ teaspoons baking soda
1 teaspoon salt, or to taste
12-ounce package chocolate chips

Preheat oven to 375°F.

Blend the carrots, sugars, butter or margarine, vanilla and eggs very well, and then add the flours, baking soda and salt, making sure that all are well-blended. Fold in the chocolate chips.

Drop the dough by rounded teaspoonsful onto cookie sheets, and bake until light brown, about 10 minutes.

Cool slightly and remove from cookie sheets to a cake rack to continue cooling.

CALIFORNIA CUPCAKES

PREPARATION: 15 MINUTES   **BAKING: 25-30 MINUTES**   **YIELD: 24 CUPCAKES**

Both carrots and pecans are products of sunny California and they go well together in this cupcake recipe.

2 cups flour
½ teaspoon allspice
4 teaspoons baking powder
½ teaspoon salt, or to taste
⅔ cup sugar
⅔ cup brown sugar, packed

½ cup soft butter or margarine
2 eggs
⅔ cup crushed pineapple, drained
1 cup cooked mashed carrots
1 cup pecans, chopped

Preheat oven to 350°F.

In a large mixing bowl combine the flour, allspice, baking powder and salt. Set the mixture aside.

In another large bowl beat together the sugars and the butter or margarine until they are light and fluffy, and then add the eggs, pineapple, and carrots and blend well.

Add the dry ingredients to the carrot mixture and mix thoroughly. Fold in the pecans.

Spoon the batter into paper-lined or well-oiled muffin tins. Bake for about 30 minutes, or until a cake tester inserted in the center comes out clean.

Cool on a rack and either frost the cupcakes or leave them plain.

CARROT/OATMEAL COOKIES

PREPARATION: 20 MINUTES   BAKING: 12-15 MINUTES   YIELD: ABOUT 7 DOZEN COOKIES

Full of nutritious carrots, bursting with beta-carotene, these cookies would keep well in a cookie jar... if you could hide the jar away where no one could find it. If you are able to put a dozen or so away, you'll find they freeze well and thaw quickly.

1 cup honey
1 cup vegetable oil
1 teaspoon vanilla extract
2 eggs
2 cups whole-wheat flour
2 teaspoons baking powder
1 teaspoon salt, or to taste

1½ teaspoons cinnamon
1 teaspoon nutmeg
1 teaspoon allspice
2 cups old-fashioned oatmeal
1 cup chopped nuts
2 cups raisins
2 cups grated carrots

Preheat oven to 375°F.

In a medium bowl beat together the honey, oil, vanilla, and eggs. In a large bowl, combine the flour, baking powder, salt, cinnamon, nutmeg, allspice, and oatmeal, and blend well. Then stir in the nuts, raisins, and carrots.

Add the liquid ingredients to the flour mixture and blend well. Drop by teaspoonsful onto an oiled cookie sheet. Bake for 12–15 minutes or until the cookies are golden brown.

Remove the cookies from the cookie sheet and cool them on a rack before storing.

CARROT DROP COOKIES

PREPARATION: 10 MINUTES   **BAKING: 12-15 MINUTES**   **YIELD 5 DOZEN COOKIES**

These golden morsels will last about as long in your cookie jar as drops of morning dew after sun-up.

1 cup butter or margarine, softened
1 cup sugar
½ cup *Carrot Marmalemon* (p. 143)

1 egg
2 cups flour
1¾ teaspoons baking powder

Preheat oven to 350°F.

In a large mixing bowl cream together the softened butter or margarine, sugar, *Carrot Marmalemon,* and egg.

In another bowl mix the flour and baking pow-

der, and then add them to the egg mixture, making sure everything is blended together well.

Drop by teaspoonsful onto oiled cookie sheets and bake for 12–15 minutes, or until golden brown. Cool on a rack.

SPICY CARROT CAKE

PREPARATION: 20 MINUTES   **BAKING: 45-60 MINUTES**   **YIELD: ONE 13" x 9" x 2" CAKE**

2 cups flour
1 teaspoon cinnamon
1 teaspoon nutmeg
2 teaspoons baking soda
1 teaspoon salt, or to taste
½ teaspoon baking powder
3 eggs

1 teaspoon vanilla
1 cup vegetable oil
1 cup granulated sugar
1 cup brown sugar, packed
2 cups grated carrots
1 cup chopped nuts

Preheat oven to 350°F.

Combine the flour, spices, soda, salt, and baking powder in a medium mixing bowl and set aside.

In a large mixing bowl, beat together the eggs, vanilla, oil, both sugars, and the shredded carrots.

Add the flour mixture to the carrot mixture and beat together until well blended. Then stir in the chopped nuts and fold to disperse them evenly throughout the batter.

Pour the batter into an oiled 13" x 9" x 2" pan and bake for 45-60 minutes or until a cake tester inserted in the center comes out clean.

SWEET CARROTY

PREPARATION: 15 MINUTES   **BAKING: 20-30 MINUTES**   **SERVES: 4-6**

This is like a crême brulée — *delicious, subtle, understated, a cross between a soufflé and a custard.*

4 egg whites
4 egg yolks
1 cup cooked puréed carrots
¼ cup brown sugar, packed

¼ teaspoon salt, or to taste
½ teaspoon orange flavoring
¼ cup slivered almonds

Preheat oven to 350°F.

In a small mixing bowl beat the egg whites until stiff peaks form. Set aside.

In a large mixing bowl, beat the egg yolks together with the carrots, brown sugar, salt, and orange flavoring.

Fold the egg whites into the carrot mixture carefully, along with the slivered almonds. Turn out into a 7-inch soufflé pan, set it in a shallow pan of hot water, and bake for 20–30 minutes, or until light and firm.

DEEP-DOWN GOOD CARROT PIE

PREPARATION: 10 MINUTES   **BAKING: 40-50 MINUTES**   **YIELD: ONE 9" PIE**

Pumpkin is not the only beta-carotene-rich vegetable that can be made into a pie.
Serve this with a generous dollop of whipped cream, whipped topping, or your favorite ice cream, or gloriously and elegantly unadorned.

1 9" pie crust, unbaked
1 cup cooked, puréed carrots
1 cup milk
½ cup evaporated milk
½ teaspoon cinnamon
¼ teaspoon cloves

¼ teaspoon salt, or to taste
⅔ cup brown sugar, packed
2 eggs, beaten
½ teaspoon ginger
¼ teaspoon nutmeg

Preheat oven to 400°F.

Have the pie crust ready on hand in your refrigerator.

Combine all the other ingredients in a large mixing bowl and blend thoroughly. Pour into a prepared pastry-lined 9-inch pie pan and bake until the crust is a rich golden brown and the filling is firm. Test it by inserting a clean table knife blade into the center. The pie is done when no filling clings to it.

PIONEER CARROT PUDDING

PREPARATION: 10-15 MINUTES   **BAKING: 1½ HOURS**   **SERVES: 4-6**

2 cups cooked carrots
3 tablespoons molasses
½ teaspoon salt
⅛ teaspoon each cloves, nutmeg, allspice and
    ginger
¼ teaspoon cinnamon

1 cup sugar
1 tablespoon flour
2 eggs
1½ cups milk
½ cup raisins, nuts or dates

Preheat oven to 375°F.

Cook the carrots in a small amount of water and drain them. Purée the carrots and stir them together with the molasses, salt, spices, sugar, flour, eggs and milk, blending all the ingredients together well. Stir in the raisins. (The mixture should have the consistency of pumpkin pie filling.)

Pour into a buttered casserole (2-quart size) and bake until a knife inserted in the center comes out clean.

Serve hot or cold with or without cream or vanilla ice cream.

CRUSTLESS CARROT CHEESECAKE

PREPARATION: 15-20 MINUTES   **BAKING: 60-75 MINUTES**   **CHILLING: 3-4 HOURS**
YIELD: TWO 9″ PIES

3 8-ounce packages cream cheese
2 tablespoons butter or margarine
4 cups cooked carrots, drained
6 eggs
1 cup brown sugar, packed
¼ cup flour
1 teaspoon cinnamon

½ teaspoon vanilla
⅛ teaspoon nutmeg
Topping:
1 cup commercial sour cream
2 tablespoons granulated sugar
¼ teaspoon vanilla
½ teaspoon nutmeg

Preheat oven to 325°F.

Bring the cream cheese to room temperature and set it aside.

Spread the butter or margarine smoothly around the inside of two pie plates or other good-sized shallow baking dishes. Set aside.

Purée the cooked, drained carrots in a blender or processor, add the eggs, and beat until the mixture is smooth and creamy. Set aside.

In a large bowl, beat together the softened cream cheese and brown sugar. Add the flour, 1 teaspoon cinnamon, ½ teaspoon vanilla, and ⅛ teaspoon nutmeg.

Blend the cream cheese mixture with the carrot mixture until smooth, and then pour the batter into the baking dishes.

Bake for 60–70 minutes, or until a kitchen knife inserted in the center comes out clean.

Remove the cakes from the oven and cool on a rack.

Meanwhile, blend the sour cream, 2 tablespoons granulated sugar, and ¼ teaspoon of vanilla together for the topping, and spread it smoothly over the top of the cooled cakes.

Sprinkle with ½ teaspoon nutmeg and chill for 3–4 hours before serving.

COOKIES CRÉCY, CHOCOLATÉS

PREPARATION: 15-20 MINUTES   BAKING: 10-15 MINUTES   YIELD: 4-6 DOZEN COOKIES

2½ cups flour
¼ teaspoon baking soda
1 teaspoon salt, or to taste
1 teaspoon cinnamon
½ teaspoon cloves
½ cup butter or margarine, softened

1 cup brown sugar, packed
1 egg
¼ cup sour cream
2 cups grated carrots
1 cup semisweet chocolate bits
1 cup raisins

Preheat oven to 375°F.

Sift the flour, baking soda, salt, and spices together in a large mixing bowl and set aside. In another large bowl beat together the butter or margarine, sugar, egg, and sour cream, beating until they are light and fluffy. Then blend in the grated carrots and the dry ingredients and mix well. Finally, stir in the chocolate bits and raisins. Drop the mixture by teaspoonsful onto oiled baking sheets and bake for 10–15 minutes, or until the cookies are golden brown. Remove them from the cookie sheets and cool them on cake racks.

BETTY BLAIR'S CARROT PUDDING

PREPARATION: 20 MINUTES   **STEAMING: 2-3 HOURS**   **YIELD: 1½-QUART MOLD**

We were browsing through an old lined notebook in which Mother used to record information about her children, directions for darning socks, formulae for bee-sting remedies — and recipes — when we came across this one. It is copied here along with information and instructions from our own notebook. You'll find that Betty Blair's pudding is very similar to a Brown Betty or Bread Pudding. We serve it warm with vanilla or maplenut ice cream.

½ cup butter or margarine
1 cup brown sugar, packed
2 well-beaten eggs
2 cups grated carrots
1 cup raisins
1 cup currants

1 cup soft bread cubes
1 teaspoon baking powder
½ teaspoon cinnamon
½ teaspoon nutmeg
⅛ teaspoon cloves
Salt to taste

In a large mixing bowl cream together the butter or margarine and the brown sugar. Add the eggs, the carrots, raisins, currants, and bread cubes. Stir in the baking powder and the spices, along with the salt to taste, and combine all the ingredients thoroughly.

Turn the pudding mixture into a buttered mold and steam it for 2–3 hours, or until the center is firm.

A special steamer is not necessary. We use a two-quart stainless steel mixing bowl for a mold. It's just the right size to fit into one of our largest covered pots. We place the rack from our pressure cooker in the bottom of the pot.

We cover the pudding bowl with tightly crimped aluminum foil and set the bowl on the rack, pour in just enough water to cover the bottom of the pot but not enough to reach the pudding bowl, and fit the lid onto the pot tightly.

We bring the water to a boil and then turn down the heat as low as we can and still keep it boiling. We have found that it is necessary to replenish the water two or three times.

When the pudding is firm, remove the pudding mold from the steamer and allow it to stand for 10 or 15 minutes before you unmold it. Loosen it as best you can by running a metal spatula around the outside edge of the pudding. Turn it upside down on a serving plate, give it a sharp *whack* on the bottom, and hope it comes out neatly and cleanly. Sometimes it does, and sometimes it doesn't. Fortunately, its taste is not affected by its appearance.

The pudding can be served warm or cold.

CARROT RAISIN BARS

PREPARATION: 15 MINUTES   **BAKING: 25-30 MINUTES**   **YIELD: 2 DOZEN BARS**

Many of our family members think that a bar without raisins in it is a contradiction in terms. Herewith, then, is what we consider to be the best of all possible bars — full of raisins and carrots.

½ cup butter or margarine
½ cup sugar
1 cup flour
2 eggs
1 cup grated carrots
1 cup brown sugar, packed

1½ cup raisins
½ cup chopped nuts
1 teaspoon lemon flavoring
2 tablespoons flour
½ teaspoon baking powder
Dash salt, or to taste

Preheat oven to 400°F.

In a large mixing bowl cream together the butter or margarine and sugar. Add 1 cup of flour and make a soft dough. Shape the dough into a ball and then press and pat it down to cover the bottom of an 8" x 8" baking pan. Bake for 15 minutes or until golden brown.

While the dough is baking, beat the eggs and add the carrots, brown sugar, raisins, nuts, and lemon flavoring. Stir in 2 tablespoons of flour, the baking powder and the salt, and blend well.

When the dough is baked, spread the carrot mixture evenly on top, return it to the oven, and bake for 25–30 minutes.

Cool in pan, cut into bars, and serve.

CARROT NUT CAKE

1 cup soft butter or margarine
1½ cups granulated sugar
½ cup brown sugar, packed
1 teaspoon cinnamon
½ teaspoon nutmeg
2 tablespoons grated orange peel
4 eggs
Orange Glaze*

2 cups grated carrots
½ cup chopped nuts
3 cups flour
3 teaspoons baking powder
1 teaspoon salt, or to taste
⅔ cup orange juice
1½ teaspoons orange flavoring

Preheat oven to 350°F.

In a large bowl cream the butter or margarine and sugars. Add the cinnamon, nutmeg and orange peel. Beat in the eggs one at a time, and stir in the orange flavoring, carrots and nuts.

Mix together the flour, baking powder and salt; add alternately with the orange juice to carrot mixture.

Turn into an oiled and floured tube pan and bake for 60 minutes, or until a tester inserted in the center comes out clean.

Invert the pan and allow the cake to cool completely. Then turn it out of the pan onto a wire rack.

Spoon Orange Glaze over the top, letting it run down the sides of the cake. Decorate with freshly grated carrot.

*ORANGE GLAZE

PREPARATION: 5 MINUTES

1¼ cups powdered sugar
1 tablespoon soft butter or margarine

¼ teaspoon orange flavoring
2-3 tablespoons orange juice

In a small bowl, beat the sugar with the butter or margarine and orange flavoring, adding enough orange juice to make a slightly runny glaze. Spoon over the cake.

CARROTY CHOCOLATE BARS

3"∠4" ?

Good flavor and pleasing texture combine in these chewy bars, made with two cups of carrots.

2½ cups flour
¼ cup cocoa
2 teaspoons baking soda
1 teaspoon allspice
1 teaspoon cinnamon
1 teaspoon salt, or to taste
½ cup granulated sugar
1 cup brown sugar, packed

½ cup butter or margarine, softened
½ cup vegetable oil
½ cup buttermilk or soured milk
3 eggs
1 teaspoon vanilla
2 cups grated carrots
1 cup grated coconut
1 cup semisweet chocolate pieces

Preheat oven to 325°F.

In a large mixing bowl combine the flour, cocoa, soda, allspice, cinnamon, and salt. Set aside.

In another large bowl, beat together the granulated sugar, brown sugar, butter or margarine, and oil until they are well blended. Add the buttermilk or soured milk, eggs, and vanilla, blending thoroughly.

Combine the egg mixture with the flour mixture until you have a smooth, lump-free batter. Then fold in the carrots and coconut, being careful to blend them evenly throughout the batter.

Pour the batter into two oiled 8" x 8" x 2" baking pans and spread it evenly. Sprinkle the top with chocolate pieces.

Bake for 35–45 minutes, or until a tester inserted in the center comes out clean. Cool on a rack, and then cut into bars.

HOLIDAY FIBER AND FRUIT CAKE

PREPARATION: 10-15 MINUTES   **BAKING: 60 MINUTES**   **YIELD: TWO 5¾" LOAVES**

This is a firm, fiber-filled fruit cake that you may want to make for holiday gift-giving. Bake it in advance, wrap it in foil, and store it in the refrigerator. Unwrap it about once a week, dribble a little brandy over it, and then close it up tightly again. By holiday time it should be well-cured and delicous.

1 cup grated carrots
1 cup water
1 cup raisins
¼ cup crushed pineapple, drained
¾ cup honey
1 cup brown sugar
1 cup granulated sugar
2 tablespoons vegetable oil
2 eggs

½ cup brandy
1 teaspoon vanilla
1½ teaspoons allspice
1 teaspoon cinnamon
1½ cups whole wheat flour
1 cup white flour
½ cup wheat germ
1 teaspoon baking soda
½ teaspoon salt, or to taste
1½ cups candied fruits

Preheat oven to 300°F.

In a medium saucepan combine the carrots, water, raisins, pineapple, honey, and sugars. Bring this mixture to a boil and cook it over medium heat for ten minutes. Remove the pan from the heat and cool it by placing it in a basin of cold water.

Meanwhile, beat together the oil, eggs, brandy, and vanilla in a large bowl. Mix the dry ingredients together in another bowl, blending them well.

Thoroughly mix and blend the egg mixture, the cooled carrot mixture, and the dry ingredients. Fold in the candied fruits.

Pour the batter into the oiled loaf pans and bake them for one hour, or until a cake tester inserted in center of the loaf comes out clean.

Cool the loaves on racks before removing them from the pans.

CARROT/PINEAPPLE CAKE

PREPARATION: 15 MINUTES　　**BAKING: 30-35 MINUTES**　　**YIELD: ONE 8" x 8" x 2" CAKE**

Although the carrot is a vegetable, its natural sweetness allows it to blend extraordinarily well with fruits — here with pineapple.

2 cups flour
1 cup sugar
1⅓ teaspoons baking powder
¼ teaspoon baking soda
1 teaspoon cinnamon
¼ teaspoon ginger
½ teaspoon salt, or to taste

¼ teaspoon cloves
1½ cups grated carrots
1 8-ounce can crushed pineapple, drained
2 eggs
½ cup vegetable oil
½ teaspoon lemon flavoring

Preheat oven to 350°F.

Mix the dry ingredients together thoroughly in a medium mixing bowl. Set aside. In another large bowl combine the carrots, pineapple, eggs, oil and lemon flavoring, beating well.

Add the dry ingredients in small amounts to the carrot mixture, blending thoroughly after each addition.

When the batter is creamy and smooth, pour it into an oiled baking pan. Bake until the cake springs back when pressed lightly, about 30–35 minutes, or until a toothpick inserted in the center comes out clean. Cool on a rack.

The cake can be frosted with a well blended mixture of: 3 ounces cream cheese, ¼ cup margarine, 1 teaspoon lemon flavoring, 2 cups powdered sugar, and enough milk to make the mixture spreadable.

MOTHER'S CARROT PUDDING

Mother's Carrot Pudding *can be served warm with cream when it is first out of the pan. Leftovers, when cooled, can be cut into slices and served with butter, margarine or cream cheese. Follow steaming directions given with* Betty Blair's Carrot Pudding *(p. 130).*

2 cups whole wheat flour
3 teaspoons baking powder
2 teaspoons cinnamon
1 teaspoon cloves
1 teaspoon baking soda
1 teaspoon nutmeg
1 teaspoon allspice

1½ cups raisins
1 cup currants
1 cup sugar
1 cup butter or margarine
2 cups grated carrots
2 cups grated potatoes

In a large mixing bowl combine the flour — start with 1½ cups — with the baking powder, cinnamon, cloves, baking soda, nutmeg, and allspice. Add the raisins and currants and make sure all of them are coated with the flour mixture. Set this bowl aside.

In another large bowl, cream together the sugar and the butter or margarine. Add the carrots and potatoes and blend them thoroughly.

Combine the dry ingredients with the carrot mixture. Mix them until they have the consistency of a dough for drop cookies, adding the rest of the flour if it is necessary.

Finally, turn the pudding into a buttered 2-quart mold or other suitable container and proceed according to directions on p. 130.

SWEET-TOOTH CARROT CAKE

PREPARATION: 20 MINUTES   **BAKING: 60-75 MINUTES**   **YIELD: 1 10" TUBE CAKE**

1 15¼-ounce can crushed pineapple
3 eggs
2 cups sugar
1¼ cups vegetable oil
3 cups flour
2 teaspoons baking soda

1 teaspoon salt, or to taste
2 teaspoons cinnamon
1½ cups grated carrots
1 cup chopped pecans
2 teaspoons vanilla

Preheat oven to 350°F.

Drain the crushed pineapple and set it aside.

In a large mixing bowl cream together the eggs, sugar and oil. Set aside.

In another bowl combine the flour, baking soda, salt, and cinnamon, mix well, and then add to the egg mixture, beating thoroughly.

Fold in the carrots, pineapple, nuts, and vanilla and turn the batter into an oiled and floured tube pan.

Bake for 60–75 minutes, or until a cake tester inserted in the center comes out clean. Place the cake upside down on a cake rack and remove it from the pan when it is completely cool.

MISCELLANY

CHAPTER 12

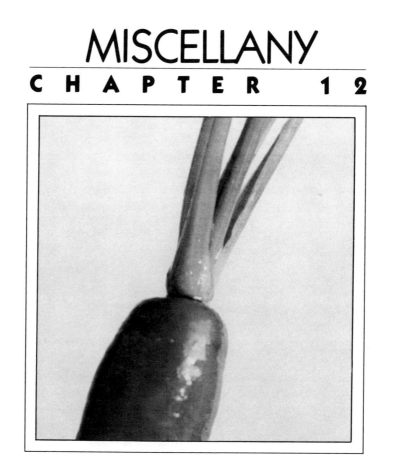

CARROT BUTTER

PREPARATION: 10 MINUTES   **COOKING: 60-75 MINUTES**   **YIELD: ABOUT 2½ CUPS**

Spread it on your toast or English muffins in the morning... combine it with peanut butter or cream cheese for sandwiches at noon... spoon it over waffles... roll it in crêpes... or stir it into ice cream. Its color is true, brilliant orange, thanks to the carrots and the oranges, and its taste is pure delight.

2 large carrots
¾ cup water
2 oranges

½ cup crushed pineapple, drained
½-1 cup sugar, or to taste

Cut carrots into thin coins and place in medium saucepan with water and bring to boil.

Peel the oranges, remove all the white membranes and seeds, separate them into sections, and add them to the carrot mixture.

Reduce the heat and simmer until the carrots are tender. Remove from the heat and cool, and then blend or process until smooth. Return to the saucepan, add the pineapple and ½-1 cups sugar, to taste. Cook until the mixture is of spreading consistency.

Pour into jars, glasses or jam pots and store in the refrigerator for up to two weeks. For longer storage, can and process as you would an apple butter. Follow the directions that accompany canning supplies.

(Note: Some carrots are sweeter than others; so are some oranges, and that's why the amount of sugar called for can vary. It also depends on personal taste.)

ANNA LOU'S CARROT FUDGE

PREPARATION: 30-45 MINUTES   **SERVES: 12-14**

We had to taste it to believe it, too. Anna Lou made a batch of this fudge and gave us each a piece. We could have eaten the whole plateful, without any help. Carrot fudge — it's orange.

1½ cups grated carrots
3½ cups sugar
½ cup sweetened condensed milk

½ cup water
½ tablespoon lemon flavoring

Cook the carrots, sugar, condensed milk, and water to the soft-ball stage (234 to 238 degrees F). Remove the pan from the heat, add the lemon flavoring, and cool to room temperature. Beat until the mixture is creamy.

Pour the fudge into a buttered shallow pan, pat it down to a one-inch depth, and let it cool. When it is firm, cut it into squares.

(If you want to make a little something on the side, take bets from anyone who thinks he can identify the ingredients.)

CARROT SANDWICHES

PREPARATION: 10 MINUTES   **YIELD: VARIABLE**

"Now I've seen everything!" *We can hear you saying it. But* try *this sandwich spread before you decide you need new glasses. We vouch for it.*

Grated carrots
Chopped nuts
Mayonnaise
Lemon-flavored yogurt

Whole wheat bread slices
Butter or margarine
Lettuce

Stir the carrots and nuts together in a medium mixing bowl and set aside. In a small bowl blend the mayonnaise and yogurt in amounts sufficient to moisten the carrot/nut mixture to your liking.

Combine the carrots and nuts with the mayonnaise/yogurt mixture and blend thoroughly.

Butter the slices of bread and spread them with the carrot mixture. Top each with a slice of crisp lettuce and another slice of bread, cut into four triangles, and serve.

Variation: Combine equal parts honey and extra-chunky peanut butter. Spread on buttered bread, top with grated carrots and a leaf of crisp lettuce, and cover with another slice of buttered bread.

CARROT MARMALEMON

PREPARATION: 5-10 MINUTES   COOKING: 60-90 MINUTES   YIELD: ABOUT 1½ CUPS

This jam is very versatile — it is delicious as a spread for breakfast breads, can be used to add pizzazz to cookies (see p. 125), and, heated slightly, makes a super sauce for vanilla ice cream.

1½ lemons, including peel
2 cups grated carrots
1½ cups sugar

½ cup water
½ teaspoon cinnamon
¼ teaspoon cloves

Cut the lemons into eighths and combine them with the carrots, sugar and water in a saucepan. Bring this to a boil, reduce the heat, and simmer until the mixture begins to thicken. Remove the pan from the heat and cool it enough to put in a blender or food processor. Chop until the mixture is close to a spreading consistency.

Return the mixture to the pan, add the cinna-mon and cloves, and simmer slowly until thick, stirring frequently to prevent sticking. If you think it needs it, add a little more water.

Pour the jam into jars or jelly pots and store in the refrigerator. It should keep well for up to two weeks. Or fill and seal small, sterilized canning jars according to the directions that come with the jars.

MRS. HUTCHINGS'S MARMALADE

PREPARATION: 50-60 MINUTES   **COOKING: 60-70 MINUTES**   **YIELD: THREE PINTS**

Nobody but you will know that there are healthful, beta-carotene-rich carrots in this marmalade. The recipe calls for enough to can. Cut it in half for smaller amounts. It keeps well in the refrigerator for up to two weeks, but we've found that ours doesn't usually last that long. Even people who don't like marmalade love this marmalade.

1 orange
2 lemons
2 cups ground carrots
Orange juice

Lemon juice
Water
Sugar

Squeeze the orange and the lemons and set the juice aside. Grind the orange rind and the lemon rinds in a food chopper or processor and then cook them in enough water to cover them until they're tender.

While the rinds are cooking, grind or chop the carrots just as you did the rinds and then add them to the pot and cook them until they are tender.

Finally, add the reserved orange and lemon juice. When the carrots are tender, remove the pan from the heat.

Measure the cooked carrot and fruit mixture and add an equal amount of water to it. For each cup of this water/fruit/carrot mixture, add two-thirds cup of sugar.

Return the pan to the stove and bring the mixture to a boil, stirring constantly. Cook the mixture for about one hour, or until the syrup reaches the jelly stage.

(You'll recognize that stage when the syrup "sheets" off the spoon instead of just running off it in a thin steady flow.)

When the syrup is jelly-like, take the pan off the stove and pour the marmalade into jelly glasses or canning jars. Process them according to the directions provided with your canning supplies.

If you halved the recipe, pour some of the marmalade into jelly or jam pots and store them in the refrigerator, or, fill air-tight containers ¾ full with any you think won't be used up right away, and freeze them for later use.

WAFFLES CRÉCY

We've had waffles every Sunday morning for so long, we don't think we could get through a weekend without them. Since we've been adding carrots to the batter, we feel quite virtuous as we slather on the butter and pour on the syrup.

2 eggs, beaten
1¾ cups milk
½ cup vegetable oil
1 teaspoon vanilla

¼ cup dried carrot flakes
2 cups flour
3 teaspoons baking powder*
½-1 teaspoon salt, or to taste

Preheat waffle iron.

Mix the eggs, milk, vegetable oil, and vanilla together well.

Stir in the carrot flakes, flour, baking powder, and salt, and blend thoroughly.

Pour onto the waffle grids and bake until golden brown.

(Note: For even fluffier waffles, separate the egg yolks and whites. Beat the whites until they are stiff and fold them into the finished batter just prior to baking.)

*If you substitute buttermilk for regular milk, decrease the baking powder to 2 teaspoons, and add 1 teaspoon baking soda.

THE RIGHT STUFFING

Once you've tried this brightly colored, good-tasting stuffing, you may never go back to dull, stodgy traditional types. This zingy dish adds interest to any kind of fowl, fish or red meat.

¼ cup butter or margarine
1 cup grated carrots
¼ cup minced onions
⅓ cup minced celery
3 cups broken corn bread

½ teaspoon salt, or to taste
Dash pepper
½–¾ teaspoon rubbed sage
½ teaspoon poultry seasoning
1 cup hot beef or chicken broth

Preheat oven to 375°F.

Melt the butter or margarine in a small saucepan, add the carrots, onions and celery, and sauté until tender.

Meanwhile, break the corn bread into a good-sized mixing bowl and sprinkle over it the salt, pepper, sage, and poultry seasoning. Toss the broken bread with the seasonings.

Finally, dribble the hot broth a little at a time over the bread mixture, tossing as you would a green salad.

(If you are going to use the stuffing to *stuff* something — like a chicken or a pork chop, for instance — you won't want to use the whole cup of broth. But, if you are making the stuffing for use as a side dish, baking it in a casserole, you will need all the moisture the recipe calls for.)

We advise covering the casserole and baking it for 20–30 minutes. This makes it crusty around the edges and tender in the center.

You can also cook this on top of the stove, just as you do other stuffings.

APPENDIXES

ESTRAGON: (VIOLENTLY) J'ai faim! (I'm hungry!)

VLADIMIR: Veux-tu une carrote? (Do you want a carrot?)

ESTRAGON: Il n'y a pas autre chose? (Isn't there anything else?)

VLADIMIR: Je dois avoir quelques navets. (I might have some turnips.)

ESTRAGON: Donne-moi une carotte.... (Give me a carrot.)

VLADIMIR: Elle est bonne, ta carotte? (Is your carrot good?)

ESTRAGON: Elle est sucrée. (It is sweet.)

En Attendant Godot

(Waiting for Godot)   Samuel Beckett

FITTING CARROTS INTO YOUR MEALS

Food alone can't make you healthy — even if you eat all the carrots you can hold, every day. But good eating habits, moderation, and variety, along with regular physical activity, will certainly help.

Nutritionists recommend that we eat a wide variety of foods in order to maintain good health. The menus here are based on nutritional standards developed by the Department of Health and Human Services and published as "Ideas for Better Eating" by the United States Department of Agriculture in January, 1981. The booklet is available from the Superintendent of Documents, U.S. Government Printing Office, Washington, D.C. 20402.

You will find as you go through the menus that most of the dishes and/or specific items can be alternated easily with others of the same types for the sake of variety.

We have not specified the kinds of milk that are available for your choice, ranging from skim to 2 percent fat to whole milk. Some of you may have to avoid whole milk because of concern about cholesterol; others may want to use skim milk because of concern about obesity.

The choice between margarine and butter is left up to you for the same reasons.

Experts advise the use of some animal-derived fats such as butter, cream, or the like with carrots and other foods rich in beta-carotene. Such fats are thought to aid in our bodies' absorption of beta-carotene, which is fat-soluble. However, cholesterol and/or weight concerns may override that consideration for some.

The menus were prepared with healthy adults in mind and should be suitably adapted for any other use, such as for young children, nursing mothers or pregnant women. If you have any condition requiring a special diet or avoidance of certain foods, or any questions at all about your particular nutrition or health needs, consult your physician.

The menus beginning on p. 150 are examples we have modified from the original U.S.D.A. publication. They can and should be adapted to your own eating habits and food choices. They are simply and only examples — not prescriptions. They are meant to be representative of the kinds of meals it is good to include in your diet on a regular basis, with special emphasis on carrots.

Our focus throughout is on beta-carotene-rich foods. Charts showing the beta-carotene content of the best sources of that nutrient in vegetables and fruits can be found in the section titled "Calculating Beta-Carotene" beginning on p. 159.

SAMPLE MENUS

BREAKFAST
1 orange, sectioned
Egg(s), soft-cooked
Twice Orange Loaf (see p. 117)
Milk
Water, tea, or coffee

BROWN BAG LUNCH
Tuna salad sandwich*
Apple, fresh
Carrot sticks
Milk

*2 ounces tuna, packed in water; 1 tablespoon chopped celery; 1 teaspoon chopped onion; 2 teaspoons mayonnaise; 2 slices whole wheat bread.

DINNER
Busy Day Dinner (see p. 84)
Green beans, fresh or frozen
Spinach salad
Italian dressing
Hard rolls (enriched or whole wheat)
Butter or margarine
Mix and Match Molded Salad (see p. 55)
Water, tea, or coffee

SNACKS
Carrot, celery, and green pepper sticks
Whole wheat crackers
Tomato juice
Water, tea, or coffee

DAY TWO

BREAKFAST
Strawberries, fresh or frozen
Shredded wheat w/sliced banana
Milk
Sugar
Water, tea, or coffee

FAST FOOD LUNCH
Jack's Carrot Beefburgers (see p. 91)
Cheddar cheese
Enriched or whole-wheat bun
Coleslaw, with mayonnaise-type
salad dressing
French fries
Apricot or peach nectar

DINNER
Chicken Coloratura (see p. 77)
Noodles or rice
Zucchini, cooked fresh
Mixed greens salad*
Italian bread (enriched or whole-wheat)
Butter or margarine
Pear, fresh
*Lettuce, spinach, carrots, green onions, Italian dressing.

SNACKS
Graham crackers
Milk
Tangerine
Carrot sticks
Pineapple juice (unsweetened)

DAY THREE

BREAKFAST
Orange sections
Carrot Scramble (see p. 68)
Bagel
Cream cheese
Carrot Marmalemon (see p. 143)
Milk
Water, tea, or coffee

LUNCH
Chicken sandwich*
Carrots, Beans & Greens Salad (see p. 58)
Apple, fresh
Water, tea, or coffee
*Sliced chicken, lettuce, mayonnaise-type salad dressing, whole wheat bread.

DINNER
Carrot, Clam & Corn Chowder (see p. 45)
Baked fish
Broccoli spears
Calico Rice (see p. 95)
Tossed green salad*
Grapes (seedless)
Water, tea, or coffee
*Lettuce, spinach, green onions, carrots, French dressing.

SNACKS
Holiday Fiber and Fruit Cake (see p. 134)
Pear, fresh
Carrot sticks

DAY FOUR

BREAKFAST
Cantaloupe
Confetti Omeletti (see p. 68)
Cheery Carroty Corn Bread (see p. 119)
Butter or margarine
Mrs. Hutching's Marmalade (see p. 144)
Milk
Water, tea, or coffee

LUNCH
Ham and cheese sandwich*
Gold Sovereign Salad (see p. 59)
Italian dressing
Orange
Water, tea, or coffee

*1 ounce lean ham; 1 ounce natural Swiss cheese; slices rye bread; 2 teaspoons mayonnaise-type salad dressing; lettuce.

DINNER
Carroty Crackery Meat Loaf (see p. 86)
Baked potatoes
Sour cream with chives
Green peas, frozen
Whole wheat roll
Butter or margarine
Vanilla yogurt (low-fat) mixed with
strawberries, fresh or frozen, unsweetened
Water, tea, or coffee

SNACKS
Golden Carrot Nut Bread (see p. 118)
Butter or margarine
Milk or juice
Carrot sticks

DAY FIVE

BREAKFAST
Grapefruit half
Staff of Life Carrot Yeast Bread toasted (see p. 115)
Butter or margarine
Carrot Marmalemon (see p. 143)
Milk
Water, tea, or coffee

LUNCH
Tomato juice
Luncheon salad*
Cheery Carroty Corn Bread (see p. 119)
Peach, fresh
Water, tea, or coffee

*Turkey, ham, mixed greens, Swiss cheese, French dressing.

DINNER
Carrotuna Casserole (see p. 71)
Corn, fresh or frozen
Green beans, fresh or frozen
Wholesome Carrot Bread (see p. 116)
Butter or margarine
Baked apple with 2 teaspoons brown sugar
Water, tea, or coffee

SNACKS
Peanut butter sandwich*
Graham crackers
Juice, your choice
Carrot sticks

*2 slices whole wheat bread; 2 tablespoons peanut butter; 2 teaspoons **Carrot Marmalemon** (see p. 143)

DAY SIX

BREAKFAST
Orange sections
Waffles Crécy (see p. 145)
Butter or margarine
Syrup
Milk
Water, tea, or coffee

LUNCH
Cream of Carrot Soup (see p. 40)
Hard rolls
Butter or margarine
Fresh fruit cup*
Milk

*Oranges, apples, bananas.

DINNER
Rolled roast of beef (lean only)
Sweet potatoes (baked)
Collard greens, fresh or frozen
Tossed salad*
Crustless Carrot Cheesecake (see p. 128)
Water, tea, or coffee

*Lettuce, tomato, green onions, carrots, Italian salad dressing.

SNACKS
Graham crackers
Apple, fresh
Juice, your choice
Carrot sticks

DAY SEVEN

BREAKFAST
Pineapple chunks
Oatmeal with cinnamon and raisins
Brown sugar
Milk
Water, tea, or coffee

LUNCH
Rich-as-Croesus Soup *(see p. 42)*
Chicken-salad-stuffed tomato*
Lemon sherbet
Water, tea, or coffee

*2 ounces cooked chopped chicken; 1 tablespoon chopped celery; 1 teaspoon chopped onion; 2 teaspoons mayonnaise; 1 medium tomato.

DINNER
Carrot-Beef Sukiyaki *(see p. 89)*
Rice
Baked apple
Water, tea, or coffee

SNACKS
Jack Robinson Carrot Bread *(see p. 116)*
Milk
Orange sections
Carrot sticks

NUTRITIONAL GUIDELINES

INTERIM DIETARY GUIDELINES — COMMITTEE ON DIET, NUTRITION AND CANCER

1. There is sufficient evidence that high fat consumption is linked to increased incidence of certain common cancers (notably breast and colon cancer) and that low fat intake is associated with a lower incidence of these cancers. The committee recommends that the consumption of both saturated and unsaturated fats be reduced in the average U.S. diet. An appropriate and practical target is to reduce the intake of fat from its present level (approximately 40%) to 30% of total calories in the diet. The scientific data do not provide a strong basis for establishing fat intake at precisely 30% of total calories. Indeed, the data could be used to justify an even greater reduction. However, in the judgment of the committee, the suggested reduction (i.e., one-quarter of the fat intake) is a moderate and practical target, and is likely to be beneficial.

2. The committee emphasizes the importance of including fruits, vegetables, and whole grain cereal products in the daily diet. In epidemiological studies, frequent consumption of these foods has been inversely correlated with the incidence of various cancers. Results of laboratory experiments have supported these findings in tests of individual nutritive and non-nutritive constituents of fruits (especially citrus fruits) and vegetables (especially carotene-rich and cruciferous vegetables).

These recommendations apply only to foods as sources of nutrients — not to dietary supplements of individual nutrients. The vast literature examined in this report focuses on the relationship between the consumption of foods and the incidence of cancer in human populations. In contrast, there is very little information on the effects of various levels of individual nutrients on the risk of cancer in humans. Therefore, the committee is unable to predict the health effects of high and potentially toxic doses of isolated nutrients consumed in the form of supplements.

3. In some parts of the world, especially China, Japan, and Iceland, populations that frequently consume salt-cured (including salt-pickled) or smoked foods have a greater incidence of cancers at some sites, especially the esophagus and the stomach. In addition, some methods of smoking and pickling foods seem to produce higher levels of polycyclic aromatic hydrocarbons and N-nitroso compounds. These compounds cause mutations in bacteria and cancer in animals, and are suspected of being carcinogenic in humans.

Therefore, the committee recommends that the consumption of foods preserved by salt-curing (including salt-pickling) or smoking be minimized.

4. Certain non-nutritive constituents of foods, whether naturally occurring or introduced inadvertently (as contaminants) during production, processing, and storage, pose a potential risk of cancer to humans. The committee recommends that efforts continue to be made to minimize contamination of foods with carcinogens from any source. Where such contaminants are unavoidable, permissible levels should continue to be established and the food supply monitored to assure that such levels are not exceeded. Furthermore, intentional additives (direct and indirect) should continue to be evaluated for carcinogenic activity before they are approved for use in the food supply.

5. The committee suggests that further efforts be made to identify mutagens in food and to expedite testing for their carcinogenicity. Where feasible and prudent, mutagens should be removed or their concentration minimized when this can be accomplished without jeopardizing the nutritive value of foods or introducing other potentially hazardous substances into the diet.

6. Excessive consumption of alcoholic beverages, particularly combined with cigarette smoking, has been associated with an increased risk of cancer of the upper gastrointestinal and respiratory tracts. Consumption of alcohol is also associated with other adverse health effects. Thus, the committee recommends that if alcoholic beverages are consumed, it be done in moderation.

The committee suggests that agencies involved in education and public information should be encouraged to disseminate information on the relationship between dietary and nutritional factors and the incidence of cancer, and to publicize the conclusions and interim dietary guidelines in their report. It should be made clear that the weight of evidence suggests that what we eat during our lifetime strongly influences the probability of developing certain kinds of cancer but that it is not now possible, and may never be possible, to specify a diet that protects all people against all forms of cancer. The cooperation of the food industry should be sought to help implement the dietary guidelines described above.

Since the current data base is incomplete, future epidemiological and experimental research is likely to provide new insights into the relationship between diet and cancer. Therefore, the committee suggests that the National Cancer Institute establish mechanisms to review these dietary guidelines at least every five years.

The Committee on Diet, Nutrition and Cancer
Assembly of Life Sciences
National Research Council
National Cancer Institute

NUTRITIONAL GUIDELINES OF THE AMERICAN CANCER SOCIETY

1. Avoid obesity.

2. Cut down on total fat intake.

3. Eat more high fiber foods, such as fruits, vegetables and whole grain cereals.

4. Include foods rich in vitamins A and C in the daily diet.

5. Include cruciferous vegetables, such as cabbage, broccoli, Brussels sprouts, kohlrabi and cauliflower in the diet.

6. Be moderate in consumption of alcoholic beverages.

7. Eat sparingly of salt-cured, smoked and nitrite-cured foods.

In regard to other nutritional factors, the ACS calls attention to seven additional dietary factors regarding which it says evidence of influence on cancer remains inconclusive:

1. *Food additives:* Those already found to cause cancer are banned. Some others may protect against the disease.

2. *Vitamin E:* There is no evidence that vitamin E prevents cancer in humans although antioxidants such as vitamin E have been shown to prevent some cancers in animals.

3. *Selenium:* Evidence that selenium protects against cancer is not strong enough to justify recommending its use. Because of the danger of selenium poisoning, the Society warns against medically unsupervised use of selenium as a food supplement.

4. *Artificial sweeteners:* The long-term effects of new noncaloric sweeteners have not yet been studied. Although saccharin at high levels has been shown to cause bladder cancer in rats, there is no clear evidence that its moderate use causes cancer in humans. Of possible concern, however, is the consumption of saccharin by children and pregnant women.

5. *Coffee:* Although some epidemiologic studies implicate high intake of coffee in bladder and pancreas cancer, research findings do not justify recommending against its moderate use.

6. *Meat and fish cooked at high temperatures, such as by frying or broiling:* Recent studies have demonstrated that high temperatures of frying or broiling create mutagens which can induce cancer in animal tests, and the subject is being studied further.

7. *Cholesterol:* Evidence relating both high and low blood cholesterol levels to human cancers is inconclusive.

Reprinted with permission of The American Cancer Society.

CALCULATING BETA-CAROTENE

Beta-carotene values can be expressed in International Units (IU) to correspond to the standard practice of measuring vitamin A, of which beta-carotene is the source, or "precursor."

The formula for such valuation is as follows:

One IU of vitamin A is equal to .3 micrograms. (A microgram is one-millionth of a gram.)

One IU of beta-carotene is equal to .6 micrograms.

If a food is known to contain a certain number of IU of vitamin A, the number of IU of beta-carotene can be arrived at by *dividing* the vitamin A IU number by 1.67.

If, on the other hand, the number of IU of beta-carotene is known, as in the charts on pages 160-163 showing fruits and vegetables high in beta-carotene, is known the number of IU of vitamin A can be calculated by *multiplying* the beta-carotene IU number by 1.67.

For example: One cup of canned, sliced carrots, which have been drained before measurement, has 13,922 IU of beta-carotene.

$$13,922 \times 1.67 = 23,250$$

Thus, it takes only 13,922 IU of beta-carotene to equal 23,250 IU of vitamin A.

We have arbitrarily excluded some fruits and vegetables from these charts because their beta-carotene is minimal, compared to amounts contained in carrots, cantaloupes, sweet potatoes, apricots and others. For more information on the nutritive value (including vitamin A/beta-carotene content) of most foods, write for Home and Garden Bulletin Number 72, which is available from the Superintendent of Documents, U.S. Government Printing Office, Washington, D.C. 20402.

VEGETABLES HIGHEST IN BETA-CAROTENE

VEGETABLE	PREPARATION	AMOUNT	BETA-CAROTENE (I.U.s)*
CARROTS	Dehydrated	3.5 ounces	59,880
	Raw — scraped, whole	1 medium	4,749
	Raw — grated	1 cup	7,246
	Cooked — diced, drained	1 cup	9,749
	Canned — sliced, drained solids	1 cup	13,922
	Baby food — strained or junior	1 ounce	2,210
SWEET POTATO (About 5" x 2")	Baked — in skin, peeled	1 potato	5,527
	Boiled — in skin, peeled	1 potato	7,150
	Candied — 2½" x 2" piece	1 piece	3,964
	Canned — solid pack, mashed	1 cup	11,910
	Canned — vacuum pack, pieces	1 piece	1,868
SPINACH	Raw — chopped	1 cup	2,670
	Cooked — drained, from raw	1 cup	8,730
	Cooked — drained, from frozen	1 cup	9,700
	Canned — drained solids	1 cup	9,820
PUMPKIN	Cooked	1 cup	9,389
COLLARDS	Cooked & drained:		
	from raw leaves only	1 cup	8,874
	from frozen, chopped	1 cup	6,922
DANDELION GREENS	Cooked & drained	1 cup	7,359
TURNIP GREENS	Cooked & drained:		
	from raw, leaves and stems	1 cup	4,952
	from frozen, chopped	1 cup	6,820

VEGETABLE	PREPARATION	AMOUNT	BETA-CAROTENE
KALE	Cooked & drained:		
	from raw, leaves w/out stems and ribs	1 cup	5,467
	from frozen, leaf-style	1 cup	6,383
VEGETABLES, MIXED	Frozen & cooked:	1 cup	5,395
SQUASH (Winter, all varieties)	Baked & mashed	1 cup	5,155
MUSTARD GREENS	Cooked & drained, w/out stems and ribs	1 cup	4,862
BEET GREENS	Cooked & drained, leaves and stems	1 cup	4,431
CABBAGE (White mustard, Bokchoy or Pakchoy)	Cooked & drained	1 cup	3,156
BROCCOLI	Cooked & drained:		
	from raw	1 stalk	2,695
	from raw, in ½" pieces	1 cup	2,323
	from frozen, chopped	1 cup	2,880
TOMATOES	Raw — medium size	1 tomato	665
	Canned — solids and liquids	1 cup	1,299
	Catsup	1 cup	2,287
	Juice — canned	1 cup	1,162
	Juice — canned	6-ounce glass	874
LETTUCE (Raw)	Butterhead (Boston type)	1 head	946
	Crisphead (Iceberg type)	1 head	1,066
	Looseleaf (Bunching varieties, including romaine, cos)	1 cup	629
ASPARAGUS (Green)	Cooked & drained, cuts and tips:		
	from raw	1 cup	784
	from frozen	1 cup	916

VEGETABLE	PREPARATION	AMOUNT	BETA- CAROTENE
PEPPERS (Hot red, w/out seeds)	Dried — ground chili powder, added seasonings	1 teaspoon	778
PEAS (Green)	Canned — whole drained solids Fresh/frozen — cooked, drained	1 cup 1 cup	701 575

*I.U.s = International Units

FRUITS HIGHEST IN BETA-CAROTENE

FRUIT	PREPARATION	AMOUNT	BETA-CAROTENE (I.U.s)*
APRICOTS	Raw — w/out pits	3 apricots	1,730
	Canned — in heavy syrup	1 cup	2,689
	Dried — uncooked	1 cup	8,485
	Dried — cooked, unsweetened, fruit and liquid	1 cup	4,491
	Nectar — canned	1 cup	1,425
CANTALOUPE (Deep orange-fleshed)	Fresh	½ melon	5,533
PEACHES (Yellow-fleshed)	Raw — whole, peeled	1 peach	796
	Raw — sliced	1 cup	1,353
	Canned — solids and liquids: syrup pack	1 cup	659
	water pack	1 cup	659
	Dried — uncooked	1 cup	3,737
	Dried — cooked, unsweetened, halves and juice	1 cup	1,826
	Frozen — sliced, sweetened, 10-ounce container	1 container	1,108
	Cup	1 cup	976

FRUIT	PREPARATION	AMOUNT	BETA-CAROTENE
PLUMS (Prune type)	Canned — light syrup pack, w/pits and liquid	1 cup	1,874
WATERMELON	Raw — 4" x 8" wedge	1 wedge	1,503
PAPAYA	Raw	1 cup	1,467
CHERRIES (Sour, tart, red)	Canned — pitted, water pack	1 cup	994
	Raw	10 cherries	42
ORANGES	Juice:		
	Frozen, concentrate, undiluted	6-ounce can	970
	Diluted w/3 parts water	1 cup	323
	Fresh	1 cup	300
	Canned, unsweetened	1 cup	300
	Dehydrated crystals, mixed with water	1 cup	300
	Raw, whole, w/out peel, seeds, 2⅝" dia.	1 orange	156
PRUNES	Cooked — sunsweetened, fruit and liquid	1 cup	922
TANGERINES	Juice — canned, sweetened	1 cup	623
	Raw, whole, w/out peel, 2⅜" dia.	1 tangerine	216

*I.U.s = International Units

Note: The above figures include all carotenes. Beta-carotene predominates; Alpha and other carotenes are trace elements. Multiply any carotene figure by 1.67 to get the equivalent in International Units of vitamin A.

Information compiled from U.S. Department of Agriculture Home and Garden Bulletin No. 72, "Nutritive Value of Foods."

INDEX